THE BEST OF

Christmas is Coming!

Ornaments and More for Kids to Make

Compiled and Edited by Linda Baltzell Wright

Oxmoor House®

page 90

©1997 by Oxmoor House, Inc.
Book Division of Southern Progress Corporation
P.O. Box 2463, Birmingham, AL 35201

Published by Oxmoor House, Inc., and Leisure Arts, Inc.

Library of Congress Catalog Card Number: 97-65260
ISBN: 0-8487-1606-X
Softcover ISBN: 0-8487-4137-4
ISSN: 0883-9077
Manufactured in the United States of America
First Printing 1997

We're Here for You!
We at Oxmoor House are dedicated to serving you with reliable information that expands your imagination and enriches your life. We welcome your comments and suggestions. Please write us at:

Oxmoor House, Inc.
Editor, *The Best of Christmas is Coming!*
2100 Lakeshore Drive
Birmingham, AL 35209

To order additional copies of this publication or any others, call 1-205-877-6560.

Editor-in-Chief: Nancy Fitzpatrick Wyatt
Senior Crafts Editor: Susan Ramey Cleveland
Senior Editor, Editorial Services: Olivia Kindig Wells
Art Director: James Boone

The Best of Christmas is Coming!
 Ornaments and More for Kids to Make

Editor: Linda Baltzell Wright
Editorial Assistant: Laura A. Fredericks
Designer: Eleanor Cameron
Illustrators: Barbara Ball, David Morrison
Copy Editor: L. Amanda Owens
Senior Photographers: John O'Hagan, Jim Bathie
Photographers: Colleen Duffley, Beth Maynard,
  Courtland W. Richards
Photo Stylist: Connie Formby
Production and Distribution Director: Phillip Lee
Associate Production Manager: Theresa L. Beste

Contents

page 86

page 102

page 62

page 130

A Note from the Editor

When you're ready to start decorating for the holiday, you don't have to look through all your old *Christmas is Coming!* books anymore—just pull out *The Best of Christmas is Coming!*

This year we've gathered together in one volume the best ornaments and decorations from the past ten editions, over 1,000 pages of *Christmas is Coming!* All the projects still have the same great how-to illustrations and color photographs to help make it easier for you to make them. So gather your supplies and get ready, because you know *Christmas is Coming!*

Get the most from this book:

In the first chapter, **For the Tree,** you will easily find ornaments galore to make for your tree, including reindeer, *(page 72)*; stars, *(page 38)*; and silly angels, *(page 69)*. There's even a tree topper, *(page 14)*, and a simple, no-sew tree skirt, *(page 62)*.

In our second chapter, **For the Mantel,** there are stockings for your pet, *(page 110)*; wreaths, *(page 119)*; garlands, *(page 116)*; and a wooden block manger scene, *(page 94)*. An adult will need to cut the wood, but you can glue on the shapes to make the scene complete.

To welcome friends and neighbors, **For the Door** is full of ideas for decorating your doors. Make a candy garland, *(page 132)*, to string over a door. Cover a doorknob with a Christmas doormouse, *(page 130)*, or trace all the hands in your family or class to make a tree to hang on a door, *(page 142)*.

To make *The Best of Christmas is Coming!* **easier** for you to use, we've divided the projects in the book into three skill levels.

Level 1 projects are very basic. Even the youngest crafters should be able to make these with only a little guidance.

page 66

Level 2 projects are slightly more involved and may require more time to make.

page 124

Level 3 projects are the most challenging. They may require a little assistance from a grown-up. They are good projects for older children.

page 106

Your safety is very important to us. When a project contains a step that should be done by or with the help of a grown-up, we make sure to tell you in bold print.

We hope you and your parents and teachers will enjoy making the projects in this book as much as we have enjoyed putting the book together for you.

Your editor,

Linda Wright

Metric Conversion Chart

U.S. Measurement	Metric Measurement
⅛"	3 mm
¼"	6 mm
⅜"	9 mm
½"	1.3 cm
⅝"	1.6 cm
¾"	1.9 cm
⅞"	2.2 cm
1"	2.5 cm
2"	5.1 cm
3"	7.6 cm
4"	10.2 cm
5"	12.7 cm
6"	15.2 cm
7"	17.8 cm
8"	20.3 cm
9"	22.9 cm
10"	25.4 cm
11"	27.9 cm
12"	30.5 cm
36"	91.5 cm
45"	114.3 cm
60"	152.4 cm
⅛ yard	0.11 m
¼ yard	0.23 m
⅓ yard	0.3 m
⅜ yard	0.34 m
½ yard	0.46 m
⅝ yard	0.57 m
⅔ yard	0.61 m
¾ yard	0.69 m
⅞ yard	0.8 m
1 yard	0.91 m

To Convert to Metric Measurements:

When you know:	Multiply by:	To find:
inches (")	25	millimeters (mm)
inches (")	2.5	centimeters (cm)
inches (")	0.025	meters (m)
feet (')	30	centimeters (cm)
feet (')	0.3	meters (m)
yards	90	centimeters (cm)
yards	0.9	meters (m)

For the Tree

Merry Mice

Trace, cut, fold, and glue. Making these curly-whiskered fellows is easy to do!

You will need:
Pencil
Tracing paper
Colored paper
Scissors
Hole punch
Ruler
Curling ribbon
Glue stick
Black fine-tip marker

4. Fold the sides of the face up and glue them over the hole. When the glue is dry, fold the ears down. Crease and then un-fold the ears.

5. Glue the inner ears and tummy in place. Let the glue dry.

6. For whiskers, cut a 6″ piece of ribbon into three pieces. Glue the pieces to the underside of the mouse's nose, using a paper clip to hold them while the glue dries.

7. Cut a 10″ piece of ribbon for the tail. Glue the tail to the back of the mouse. Let the glue dry.

8. Using the blade of your scissors, gently curl the tail and the ends of the whiskers. Draw eyes with the marker.

1. Trace the patterns, pressing hard with your pencil.

2. Turn the tracings over and retrace them onto sheets of colored paper. Cut out the colored pieces. Cut the circle for the inner ears in half.

3. Fold the top of the mouse down and punch a hole as shown. Cut a 12″ piece of ribbon for a hanger. Pull the ribbon through the holes and tie the ends.

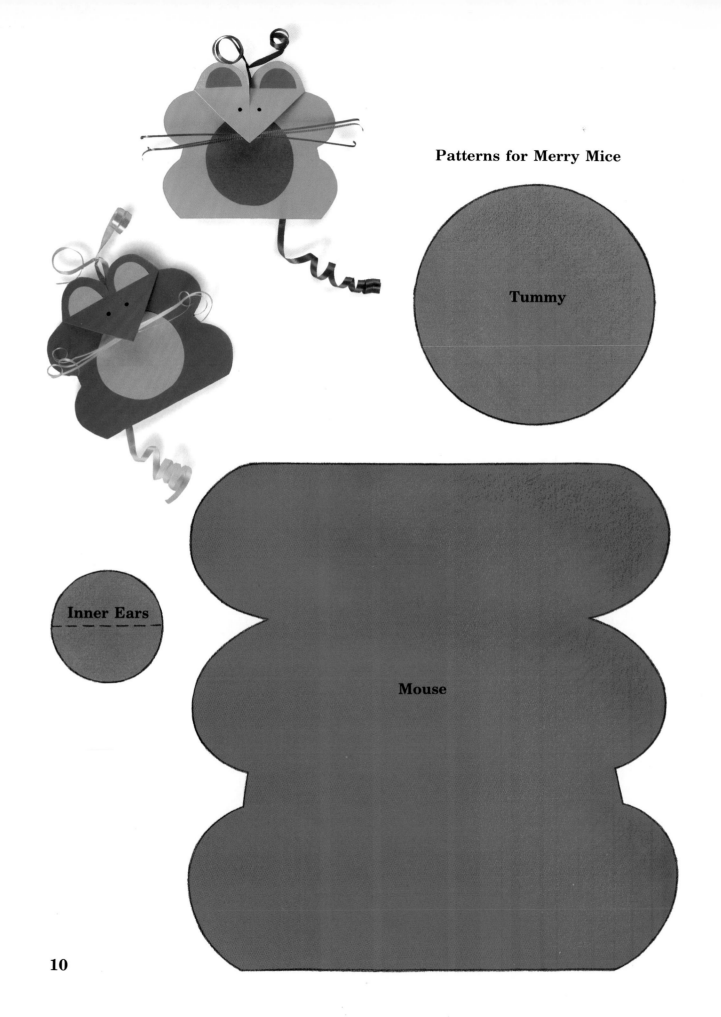

Patterns for Merry Mice

Tummy

Inner Ears

Mouse

10

Wee Weavings

How merry these will look on your tree! Combine different colors to make each one special.

You will need:
Embroidery floss in different colors
Round toothpicks
Scissors
White glue

1. Using floss that is still attached to the skein, tie two toothpicks together, making an X with the floss. Knot the floss in back of the toothpicks.

2. Follow the drawings to weave the ornament. As you weave, be sure to lay the floss next to, not on top of, the floss that is already in place.

3. When you're ready to change colors, cut the floss. Tie the second color of floss to the end of the first. Begin weaving again, keeping the knot in back.

4. Change colors as often as you like. When the toothpicks are almost covered, wrap the floss around the "top" toothpick several times. Cut the floss and glue the end to the back of the toothpick. Let dry.

5. Cut a piece of floss for a hanger. Glue the ends to the back of the top toothpick. Let the glue dry.

Level 2

Sparkly Snowmen

What makes these so lovable? Pom-pom noses, a pudgy shape, and great big toothy smiles!

You will need:
Pencil
Tracing paper
Scissors
2 (5″ x 5½″) pieces of white felt
Straight pins
Scraps of colored felt, fabric, and ribbon
Pinking shears
3 cotton balls
White glue
Small plastic buttons (or a hole punch to make felt buttons)
Small white pom-pom
Black slick pen
Clear glitter
Fishing line

1. Trace and cut out the patterns.

2. Stack the white felt pieces and pin the snowman to them. Pin the hat to a scrap of colored felt. Cut out the felt pieces. Using the pinking shears, cut the scarf from a fabric scrap.

3. Put the cotton balls on one snowman's tummy. Run a line of glue around the snowman's edges and place the other snowman on top. Pinch the edges of the snowmen together. Let the glue dry.

4. Glue the hat to the snowman's head. Cut a piece of ribbon for a hatband. Cut a tiny holly leaf and some berries from green and red felt. Glue the pieces to the hat and let dry.

5. Glue the scarf, buttons, and pom-pom nose in place. Let the glue dry.

6. Practice drawing dots on a scrap of felt, using the slick pen. Then draw two eyes and a mouth on the snowman. Let the paint dry.

7. Spread glue on the snowman and sprinkle him with glitter. When the glue is dry, shake off the excess glitter.

8. Use a pin to punch a hole in the top of the snowman's hat. Pull a piece of fishing line through the hole and tie the ends for a hanger.

Hat

Snowman

Scarf

Dip-and-Drape Angel

An ornament this sweet will be the star of any tree. Follow the steps and watch with surprise as your angel takes shape.

Before you start: The more you handle the dampened Dip-'N-Drape pieces, the less sticky they become, so dress your angel quickly. If you cannot find Dip-'N-Drape fabric, use regular fabric and liquid fabric stiffener.

You will need:
Pencil
Tracing paper
Scissors
8½″ x 10½″ white poster paper
10½″ x 17″ Dip-'N-Drape fabric
Waxed paper
Bowl of water
Toothpick
Paintbrushes
Gesso
Acrylic paint (white, blue, flesh, and
　yellow)
Fine-tip markers (blue, brown, and red)
Clear plastic spray enamel
Narrow ribbon
White glue
Gold embroidery floss (for hanger)

1. Trace and cut out the patterns. Cut out the pieces as marked.

2. Tear off small and medium-size pieces of waxed paper for stuffing the dress sleeves and skirt. Crumple the pieces.

3. Gently crumple the waxed paper face (for padding) and lay it on the poster paper angel's face. Dip the Dip-'N-Drape face quickly in water and then wrap it around the poster paper face, covering the waxed paper.

4. Line the angel's arms and body with the crumpled waxed paper. Dampen one dress piece and drape it over the angel, gathering the dress piece at the neck. Gently turn the angel over.

Line the back of the angel with crumpled waxed paper. Dampen and drape the second dress piece, overlapping the edges with the front dress piece.

5. Dampen the hair and drape it over the angel's head. Use the toothpick to separate and arrange the strands. (If a strand breaks off, just stick it back on.)

15

6. Dip the Dip-'N-Drape halo and stick it on the poster paper halo. Press the halo (Dip-'N-Drape side) onto the back of the angel's head.

7. Dip the Dip-'N-Drape wings and stick them onto the poster paper wings. Press the wings (Dip-'N-Drape side) onto the back of the angel. Let the angel dry overnight.

8. Paint the entire angel with gesso and let dry. Paint the angel with several coats of paint, using one color at a time and letting the paint dry between coats. When the angel is dry, draw the face with the markers. Spray the angel with the clear plastic enamel and let dry.

9. Tie the ribbon into a bow and glue it to the neck of the dress. Glue the ends of the floss to the back of the halo. Let the glue dry.

Angel

Cut 1 from poster paper.

16

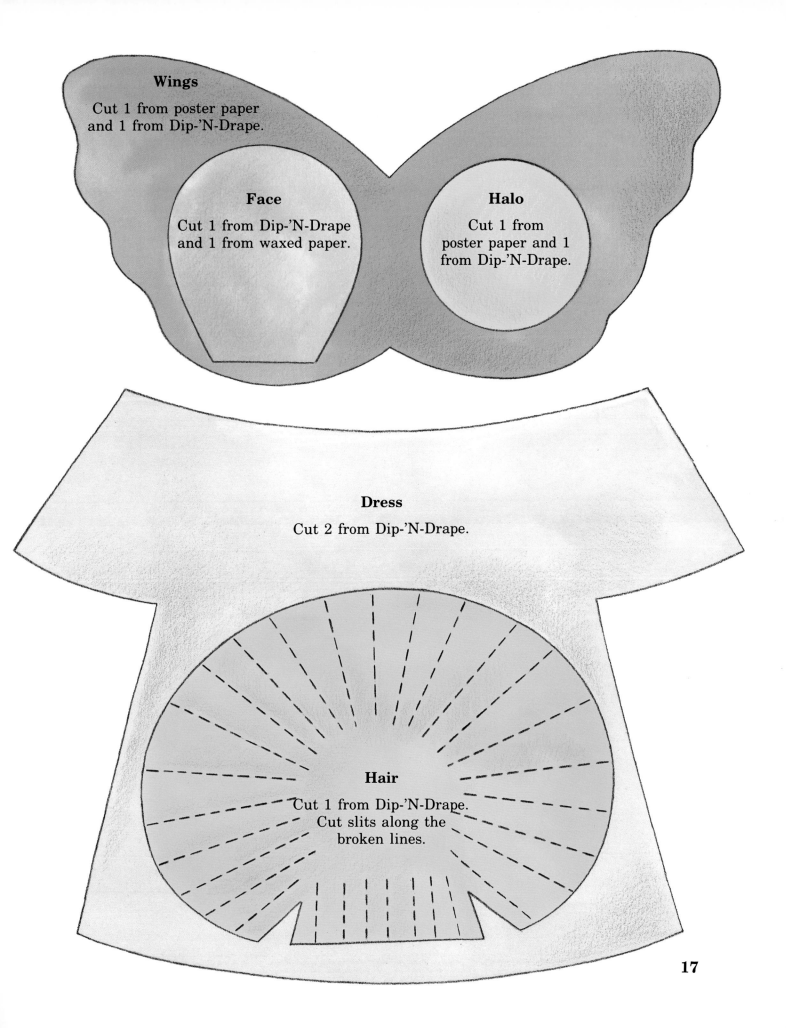

Wings

Cut 1 from poster paper and 1 from Dip-'N-Drape.

Face

Cut 1 from Dip-'N-Drape and 1 from waxed paper.

Halo

Cut 1 from poster paper and 1 from Dip-'N-Drape.

Dress

Cut 2 from Dip-'N-Drape.

Hair

Cut 1 from Dip-'N-Drape. Cut slits along the broken lines.

Powder-Puff Snowmen

Use snowy white puffs to make these folks. Cover their ears so they won't get cold!

You will need:
White glue
4 small white powder puffs
Hole punch
Scraps of felt
Scissors
Rickrack
4 small pom-poms
Ribbon bow
Scrap of fabric for scarf
Pencil
Tracing paper
Ribbon

1. Glue the edge of one powder puff over the edge of another powder puff to make the snowman's head and body. Let the glue dry.

2. Use a hole punch to make felt circles for eyes and buttons. Glue them in place. Cut out a carrot nose and glue it in place.

3. For earmuffs, glue a piece of rickrack and two pom-poms on the snowman's head. Let the glue dry.

4. For Mrs. Snowman, glue on the ribbon bow.

5. For Mr. Snowman, cut a strip for a scarf from the scrap of fabric. Tie the scarf around the snowman's neck. Glue the scarf, if you need to, to keep it in place.

Trace the patterns for the broom on tracing paper. Cut out the patterns and draw around them on felt. Cut out the felt pieces and glue them together. When the glue is dry, glue the broom to the back of Mr. Snowman.

6. Cut a piece of ribbon for a hanger. Glue the ends of the ribbon to the back of the snowman. Let the glue dry.

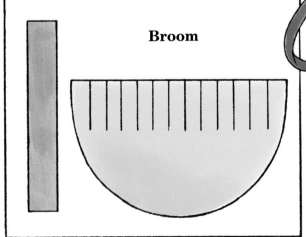

Broom

19

Shiny Shapes

Making these ornaments is as easy as counting one—two—three!

You will need:
Fine-tip marker
Tracing paper
Scissors
Vinyl in different colors
Hole punch
Toothpick
White glue
Ribbon

1. Trace the patterns for the heart, star, and tree on tracing paper. Cut out the patterns and draw around them on vinyl. Cut out the vinyl ornaments.

2. To make balls for the tree, punch holes in scraps of vinyl. Using the toothpick, put tiny dots of glue on the front of the tree. Place the balls on the dots of glue. Let the glue dry.

3. Punch a hole in the top of each ornament. For a hanger, pull the ends of a ribbon through the hole and tie a knot.

Glitter Birds

These silver birds are sweet as can be. And how they will sparkle on your Christmas tree!

You will need:
Felt-tip marker
6" square of tracing paper
Clear tape
6" square of cardboard
Plastic wrap
White glue
Tinsel cord (about 19" for each ornament)
Toothpick
Glitter
Scissors
Aluminum foil
Ribbon
Sequins
Straight pin
Fishing line

1. Using the felt-tip marker and tracing paper, trace the pattern.

2. Tape the tracing to the piece of cardboard. Cover the tracing and cardboard with plastic wrap. Tape the edges of the plastic wrap to the back of the cardboard.

3. Trace the design with a thin line of glue. Allow the glue to dry for several minutes.

4. Place the tinsel cord along the lines of glue. Hold the cord in place until the glue is slightly dry. Let the glue dry.

5. Fill the area inside the cord with glue, using a toothpick to spread the glue. Sprinkle glitter over the glue. Let the glue dry for several days.

6. When the glue is completely dry, gently peel the bird from the plastic wrap. Cut a beak from aluminum foil. Cut a piece of ribbon and tie it into a bow. Glue the beak, the bow, and a sequin eye in place. Let the glue dry.

7. Poke a hole in the top of the ornament with a straight pin. Pull a piece of fishing line through the hole and tie the ends to make a hanger.

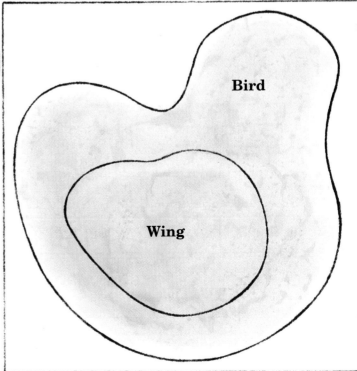

Bird

Wing

Dream Cones

Strawberry, lemon, or lime? Pick your favorite flavor. Turn sugar cones into dream cones and hang them on your tree.

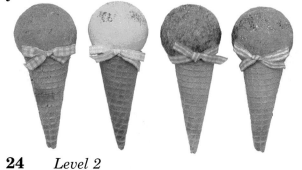

You will need (for each):
Paper cup (5-ounce size works well)
Scissors
Sugar cone
Colored tissue paper
Measuring spoons
White glue
Water
Foil pie pan
1 (2¼") plastic foam ball
Glitter
Narrow ribbon

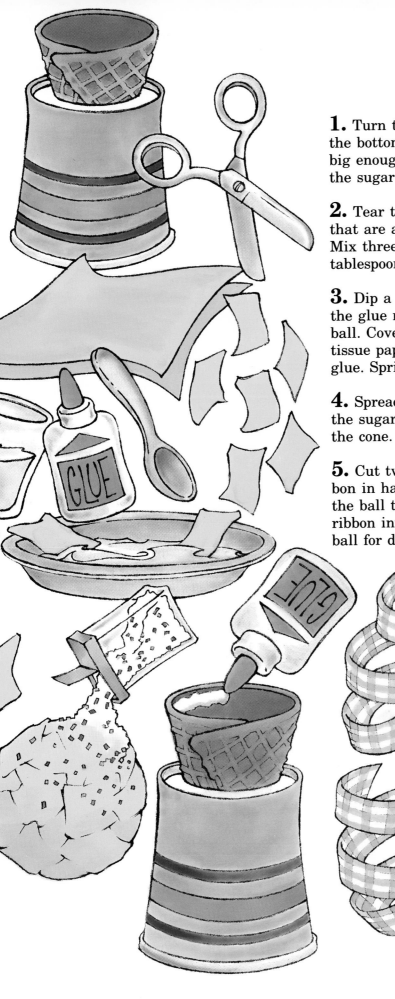

1. Turn the paper cup upside down. In the bottom of the cup, cut a hole that is big enough to hold the sugar cone. Stand the sugar cone in the hole.

2. Tear the tissue paper into little pieces that are about the size of a half-dollar. Mix three tablespoons of glue with three tablespoons of water in the foil pie pan.

3. Dip a piece of the tissue paper into the glue mixture and smooth it onto the ball. Cover the whole ball with pieces of tissue paper that have been dipped in glue. Sprinkle the ball with glitter.

4. Spread glue around the inside edge of the sugar cone. Gently push the ball into the cone. Let the dream cone dry.

5. Cut two pieces of ribbon. Fold one ribbon in half. Glue the ends onto the top of the ball to make a hanger. Tie the other ribbon into a little bow and glue it to the ball for decoration. Let the glue dry.

Picture-Perfect Wreaths

Somebody would love to have a picture of you. Can you guess who?

You will need (for each):
Pencil
Coffee cup (about 3½" across)
Felt
Pinking shears
Top to baby food jar
Scissors
Tacky craft glue
Ribbon bow
Sequins
Toothpick (for picking up sequins)
Picture
Ribbon for hanger

1. Draw around the coffee cup on felt. Using the pinking shears, cut out the felt circle.

2. Place the jar top in the center of the felt circle. Draw around the top. Using scissors, cut out the circle to make a wreath.

3. Glue the bow at the bottom of the wreath. Glue sequins for berries around the wreath. Let the glue dry.

4. Draw around the coffee cup on felt to make another circle. Use pinking shears to cut out the circle.

5. Glue the picture to the felt circle. At the top of the circle, glue the ends of the ribbon hanger. Put glue around the edges of the circle. Place the wreath on top. Let the glue dry.

27

Candy Cane Reindeer

These candy cane reindeer are so easy to make that you won't need a lick of help! Make a boxful of these famous fellows. Give them for presents or party favors, or hang them on your tree.

You will need (for each):
Candy cane
2 chenille stems
Scissors
White glue
2 plastic wiggly eyes
Red pom-pom
Ribbon
Jingle bell
Fishing line

1. To make antlers, twist one chenille stem around the curve in the candy cane. Cut the other chenille stem into two short stems. Twist the short stems around the ends of the long stem. Turn up the ends of the stems.

2. Glue the wiggly eyes and the pom-pom nose onto the candy cane.

3. Pull a ribbon through the opening at the top of the jingle bell. Tie the ribbon around the candy cane to make a bow.

4. Tie fishing line to the candy cane to make a loop for hanging.

Yarn-Wrapped Wreath

Use bright green yarn to fashion this wreath. Add shiny red buttons for berries.

You will need:
Pencil
Coffee can lid
6" square of white poster paper
Scissors
Small jar (about 2" across)
Tape measure
Thick green yarn
24" piece of ribbon
Tacky craft glue
Red buttons
Fishing line

1. Draw around the lid on poster paper. Place the jar in the middle of the circle. Draw around the jar. Cut out the circles to make a wreath.

2. Cut twelve pieces of yarn each about 18" long. Wrap one piece of yarn around the wreath, leaving 1" of yarn on the back of the wreath. Wrap another piece of yarn around the wreath, catching the 1" end of the first piece. Keep wrapping the wreath with yarn until the wreath is covered, tucking any loose ends under the wrapped yarn.

3. Tie the ribbon into a bow and glue it to the top of the wreath. Glue on the buttons for berries. Let the glue dry.

4. Cut a piece of fishing line for a hanger. Run the fishing line under some yarn at the top of the wreath and tie the ends.

Take-the-Cake Cupcakes

Little brothers and sisters can share in the fun of "cooking up" a batch of these colorful cupcakes. How yummy they look! But don't be fooled. These cakes aren't for eating—they're for trimming the tree!

For safety's sake: Ask a grown-up to help you use the electric mixer and to cut the plastic foam balls in half.

Making the Royal Icing

You will need:
A grown-up
Egg whites from 3 large eggs
½ teaspoon cream of tartar
1 (16-ounce) package powdered sugar, sifted
Large mixing bowl
Spatula
Electric mixer
4 small bowls
4 spoons
Red, green, and yellow food coloring
Plastic wrap

1. Put the egg whites in a large mixing bowl. (Warm egg whites make a bigger batch of icing than cold ones. So, if they're cold, let the egg whites sit out awhile before you beat them.)

2. Add the cream of tartar. Turn the electric mixer to medium speed and beat the egg whites until they are frothy.

3. Add some of the powdered sugar to the egg whites. Mix the sugar and egg whites on medium speed. Add more sugar and mix again. Keep adding sugar and mixing until you have added all of the sugar.

4. Beat the sugar and egg whites on medium speed until they form icing. This will take about five minutes.

5. Divide the icing into the four small bowls. Using a different spoon for each color, stir food coloring into the icing in three of the bowls. Leave one bowl of icing white. Cover the bowls with plastic wrap so that the icing will stay soft. (If it's okay with your mom, you can eat any icing that is left in the mixing bowl.)

Icing the Cupcakes

You will need (for six cupcakes):
A grown-up
6 silver foil baking cups
Muffin tin
Spoon
Royal Icing (pink, green, yellow, and white)
6 paper napkins (lunch size)
6 paper clips
3 (2½") plastic foam balls
Knife for icing the cupcakes
Little candies
Narrow ribbon

1. Put the foil baking cups into the muffin tin.

2. Place a spoonful of icing in a baking cup. Unfold a paper napkin, crumple it, and place it on top of the icing. Spread a spoonful of icing on top of the napkin.

3. **Ask the grown-up** to cut the foam balls in half. Push a paper clip a little more than halfway into the top of one of the half-balls. Hold the half-ball by the paper clip and spread the top with icing. Place the half-ball on top of the crumpled napkin.

4. Decorate the cupcake with little candies while the icing is still soft. If you use colored sugar crystals, sprinkle them on the cupcake lightly at first to make sure that the color does not run.

5. Make the rest of the cupcakes, one at a time. Leave the cupcakes in the muffin tin until the icing is hard.

6. Cut twelve pieces of ribbon. Pull one ribbon through each paper clip and knot the ends to make a hanger. Pull another ribbon through each paper clip and tie a bow.

Color Melts

Hold these ornaments up to a sunny window and watch the light filter through them. Their translucent appearance resembles stained glass but actually comes from crayon shavings melted between waxed paper.

You will need (for each ornament):
A grown-up
Tracing paper
Pencil
Scissors
Heavyweight colored paper
Masking tape
Waxed paper
Ironing board
2 cloth towels
Crayons in desired colors
Vegetable peeler
Iron
Glue
Hole punch
Scrap of satin ribbon

1. Trace and cut out the desired pattern. Fold the heavyweight paper in half and trace the pattern onto the paper.

2. Tape the 2 layers of the paper together to hold them in place. Cut along the inner and the outer edges of the design. Set the 2 shapes aside.

3. Repeat Steps 1 and 2 with the waxed paper, cutting along the **outer** edge only. Do not tape the layers together.

4. Cover the ironing board with 1 towel. Place 1 waxed paper cutout on the cloth. Remove the paper from the crayons. Using the peeler, shave different colored crayons onto the waxed paper, lightly covering the surface. (Be careful not to make a pile of shavings or your ornament will appear dark.)

Aligning the edges, place the remaining waxed paper cutout on top of the first, sandwiching the shavings in between. Place the remaining towel on top of the waxed paper and **ask the grown-up** to lightly press the 2 layers with a warm iron until the shavings are melted. Let the waxed paper cool.

5. Sandwich the waxed paper pieces between the 2 heavyweight paper shapes, aligning the edges. (Trim any excess waxed paper around the edges of the ornament.) Glue the layers together along the outer edges. Let the glue dry.

6. Using the hole punch, make a hole in the ornament where indicated.

7. For the hanger, thread the ribbon through the hole and tie the ends together in a knot.

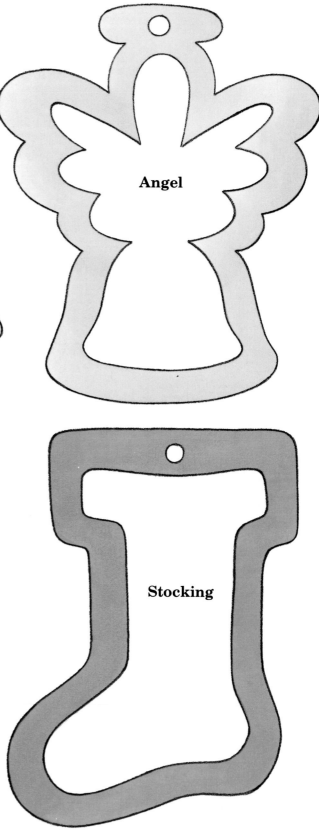

Angel

Stocking

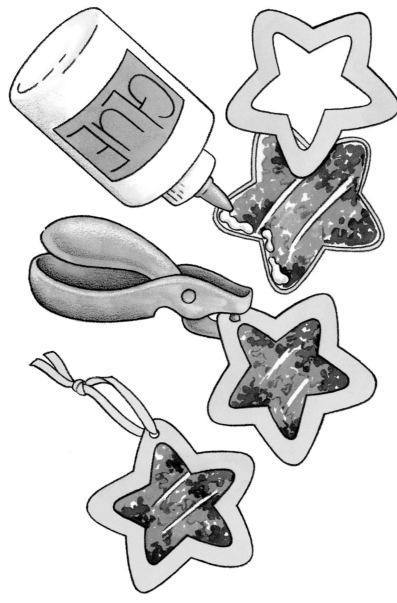

36

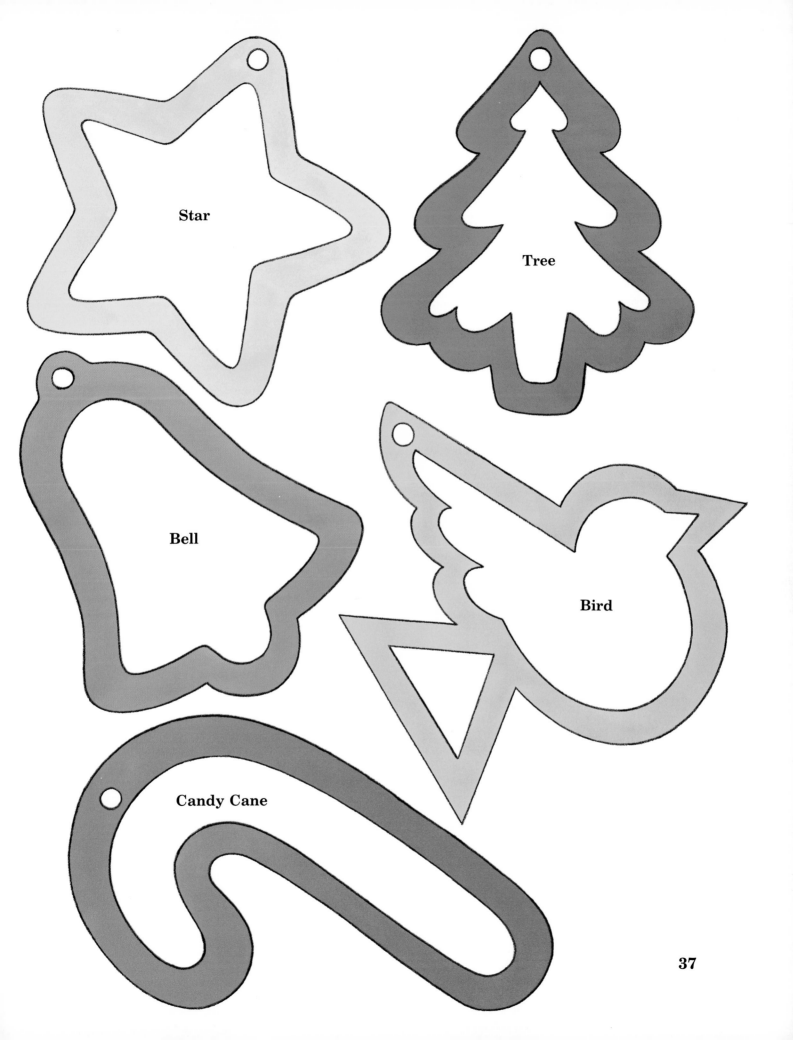

Star

Tree

Bell

Bird

Candy Cane

37

Wire Stars

Shape inexpensive coated wire into unique Christmas decorations. Tie a gold thread around the tip of the star and then hang the star on the tree or in your window. Or trim a package with this unusual topper.

You will need (for 1 star):
Tracing paper
Pencil
Block of wood measuring at least 8" x 9"
5 nails
Hammer
4' length each bell wire in 2 different colors
Wire cutters
Needlenose pliers (optional)

Note: You'll find a metric conversion chart on page 5.

1. Using the pencil, trace the star pattern onto the tracing paper. Cut out the star. Place the star pattern onto the block of wood and, using the pencil, trace the star. Number the points of the star as indicated on the pattern.

2. Hammer a nail approximately halfway into the block of wood at each point of the star. Using 1 length of wire and leaving a 10" tail, wrap the wire once around nail #1; then loop the wire around nail #2. Continue looping the wire around the nails, working in numerical order. At nail #6 twist the 2 wires together. Using the wire cutters, trim the wire ends even. Repeat, using the remaining length of wire.

2 •

5 •

4 •

Star

3 •

1 & 6 •

3. Slide the star off the nails. (If the nail heads are too large to slide the star over, use the claw end of the hammer to remove the nails from the wood.) From the excess wire, cut 5 (3") pieces. Referring to the illustration, twist 1 (3") piece around each intersection of the wires. Using the wire cutters, trim the excess wire.

4. If desired, use the needlenose pliers to bend zigzags in the tails of the star. Alternatively, trim the tails and bend the cut ends around the star.

Polka-Dot Bird

How Christmasy this perky bird looks—as if he's all dressed up for a party!

You will need:
A grown-up
Glue stick
2 (4" x 6½") pieces of polka-dot wrapping paper
4" x 6½" piece of poster paper
Pencil
Tracing paper
Scissors
Hole punch
5½" x 14" piece of tissue paper
2 round reinforcement tabs (with holes)
String

1. Glue the wrapping paper to both sides of the poster paper. Let the glue dry.

2. Trace the pattern for the bird. Cut out the pattern and draw around it on the poster paper. Cut out the bird.

3. Ask the grown-up to cut the slit in the bird for the wings. Punch a hole above the slit with the hole punch.

4. To make the wings, fold the tissue paper as though you were making a fan. Pull the wings halfway through the slit.

5. Punch a hole for the bird's eye. Stick a reinforcement tab over the hole on each side of the bird.

6. Pull the string through the hole above the wings. Tie the ends for a hanger.

Bird

Cut slit here.

Pop-Silly-Sicles

Decorate your Christmas tree with these frosty favorites—and hope that no one tries to take a bite!

You will need:
Newspaper
Scissors
Ruler
Pencil
Paper clips
Wooden craft sticks
Masking tape
Measuring spoons
Colored tissue paper
White glue
Water
Foil pie pan
Clear glitter
Ribbon

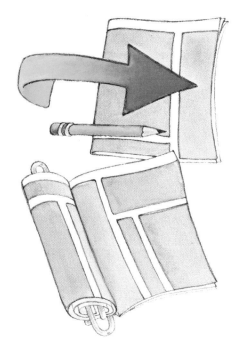

1. Take two double pages from a newspaper that your mom and dad have already read. Cut the double pages apart on the line where they have been folded so that you have four single pages.

2. Stack the pages one on top of the other. Measure and mark lines 4″ from the top and 3″ from one side of the stacked papers. Cut along the lines and then throw away the strips.

3. Fold the stacked papers in half, bringing the top edge of the papers to the bottom edge of the papers. Fold the papers in half again, the same way, bringing the top to the bottom.

4. Fold the papers in half a third time, but this time bring the left side of the papers to the right side of the papers. Rub up and down along the fold line with the side of your pencil to make a crease. This crease will be between the two sides of the pop-silly-sicle.

5. Open the paper. Roll one side of the paper toward the crease in the middle. Use paper clips to hold the roll in place. Roll the other side and clip the roll.

6. Run a long piece of masking tape down the crease between the two rolls, around the bottom, and up the back between the two rolls. Take off the paper clips. To make a hanger, tape one of the paper clips to the top of one of the rolls. Cover the rolls with strips of masking tape. In the bottom of each roll, make a cut in the tape and push a craft stick through the cut.

7. Cut the tissue paper into strips. Mix three tablespoons of glue with three tablespoons of water in the pie pan.

8. Dip the strips of tissue paper into the glue mixture, one at a time, and then smooth them onto the pop-silly-sicle. When you have covered up all of the tape, sprinkle glitter over the pop-silly-sicle. Let it dry overnight.

9. To hang the pop-silly-sicle, pull a ribbon through the paper clip and knot the ends.

Everything That Glitters

These colorful balls will add sparkle and shine to the Christmas tree, and best of all, they won't break like glass balls can!

You will need (for 1 ornament):
Waxed paper
Paper clip
Styrofoam ball of desired size
Glitter paint
Paper plate
Paintbrush
½ yard wire-edged ribbon
Thick craft glue
Scissors

1. Cover the work surface with the waxed paper.

2. For the hanger loop, push the paper clip into the top of the Styrofoam ball until only ¼" of the paper clip remains outside the Styrofoam ball.

3. Squirt a blob of glitter paint onto the paper plate. Use the paintbrush to apply the glitter paint to the Styrofoam ball. Let the paint dry. Apply a second coat of glitter paint if desired; let the paint dry.

4. Tie the ribbon into a bow. Glue the bow in front of the hanger loop. Trim the ribbon ends. Let the glue dry.

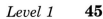

Treasures from Trash

Don't throw away those old drawings or greeting cards—recycle them and make paper ornaments or package toppers. Choose cookie cutters in unique shapes and create decorations that are environmentally friendly.

You will need (for each ornament):
A grown-up
1 sheet used construction paper or 1
    greeting card
Electric blender
2 cups warm water
Window screen
Cookie cutter in desired shape
Ribbon scrap
Thick glue
Assorted trinkets, curling ribbon, or
    costume jewels

1. Remove staples, tape, or other nonpaper items from the paper. Tear the paper into tiny pieces and place them in the blender.

2. Ask the grown-up to watch as you do this step: Pour the warm water into the blender. Place the lid on the blender and process the mixture until it becomes a thick pulp.

3. Place the window screen over a sink. Place the cookie cutter on top of the screen and fill it with the paper mixture. Let the water drain completely. Carefully remove the cookie cutter and let the ornament air dry overnight.

4. To make the hanger, fold the ribbon in half and glue the ends to the back of the ornament at the center top. Decorate the ornament as desired with the trinkets, the curling ribbon, or the jewels.

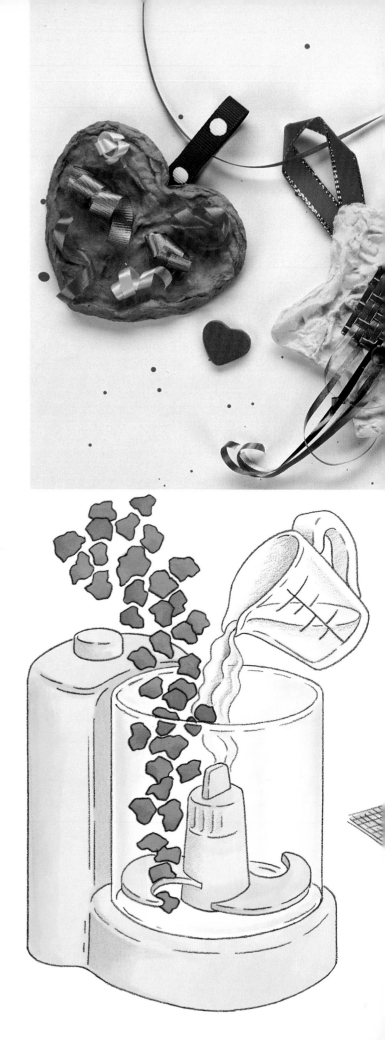

Nursery Rhyme Ornaments

Dreams of sailing a little boat out to sea by the light of the moon come alive with these cardboard ornaments. They look like they just popped out of a fantasy story!

You will need (for all 4 ornaments):
Tracing paper
Pencil
Scissors
8½" x 11" piece lightweight cardboard
Permanent markers: red, black
Glue stick
Red satin ribbon: 2⅜ yards ¼"-wide, 8"
    length ⅛" wide
2 (⅛") black shank buttons
¼"-diameter hole punch
White paint pen
Embroidery scissors

1. Trace the patterns onto the tracing paper, transferring markings. Cut them out.

2. Transfer 2 anchor patterns onto the cardboard. Transfer 1 moon pattern onto the cardboard. Reverse the moon pattern and transfer it onto the cardboard again. Transfer 2 hatbands and 2 heart cheeks onto the cardboard. Cut them out.

3. For the red ribbon moon: Using the red marker, outline 1 moon, 1 heart cheek, and 1 hatband on 1 side. Referring to the drawing, cut 5 lengths from the ¼"-wide ribbon and glue them diagonally inside the hatband area. Trim the ribbon ends even with the cardboard edges. Glue the hatband in place on the moon.

4. Referring to the drawing, cut 3 lengths from the ¼"-wide ribbon and glue them across the heart cheek. Trim the ribbon ends even with the cardboard edges. Glue the heart in place on the moon.

5. Cut a 2" length from the ⅛"-wide ribbon. Glue it in place on the moon for the mouth. Trim the ribbon end even with the cardboard edge.

49

6. Referring to the drawing, cut 3 lengths from the ¼"-wide ribbon and glue them in place on the nose of the moon. Trim the ribbon ends even with the cardboard edges.

7. Using the black marker, draw eyelashes on the moon where indicated on the pattern. Glue 1 button in the center of the eyelashes.

8. Cut 2 (1") lengths of ¼"-wide ribbon and 2 (1") lengths of ⅛"-wide ribbon. Referring to the drawing, to make the pom-pom on the moon's hat, glue the ¼"-wide ribbon lengths in an X at the tip of the moon. Glue the ⅛"-wide ribbon lengths to resemble a plus sign on top of the ¼"-wide ribbon.

9. Punch a hole in the moon where indicated on the pattern. Cut a 14" length from the ¼"-wide ribbon. Thread the ribbon through the hole and tie the ends into a bow.

10. For the white painted moon: Glue the remaining hatband and heart cheek in place on the remaining moon.

11. Referring to the photo and using the white paint pen, outline the moon, the hatband, and the heart cheek. Paint stripes inside the hatband and the heart cheek. Fill in the nose area. Paint the mouth and the eyelashes where indicated on the pattern. Let the paint dry.

12. Glue the remaining button in place in the center of the eyelashes.

13. Repeat steps 8 and 9 above to complete the white painted moon.

14. **For the red ribbon anchor:** Using the embroidery scissors, cut out the heart-shaped ribbon hole from 1 cardboard anchor, being careful not to cut into it from an outside edge. Using the red marker, outline the anchor and the hole on 1 side. Referring to the photo, cut 3 lengths from the ¼"-wide ribbon and glue them diagonally along the center part of the anchor. Trim the ribbon ends even with the cardboard edges. Cut a 14" length from the ¼"-wide ribbon. Thread the ribbon through the hole and tie the ends into a bow.

15. **For the white painted anchor:** Using the embroidery scissors, cut out the heart-shaped ribbon hole from the remaining anchor, being careful not to cut into it from an outside edge. Using the white paint pen, outline the anchor and the hole on 1 side. Let the paint dry. Cut a 14" length from the ¼"-wide ribbon. Thread the ribbon through the hole and tie the ends into a bow.

Moon

Anchor

51

Paint Stick Ornaments

Stir up some fun with these ornaments! They are a great way to recycle old paint sticks.

You will need (for each ornament):
A grown-up
1 wooden paint stick
Silver webbing
Electric drill with small bit
Craft glue
Medium-tip permanent black marker
Scissors
1 (7-mm) red pom-pom
For Santa: 2 large wooden craft sticks (tongue depressor size); masking tape; red spray paint; 4 (½" x ¾") pieces and 1 (2½"-diameter) circle white, 2 (1¼") squares and 2 (¼" x 1⅛") pieces black, and 1 (4½"-diameter) circle red felt; 1 copper brad; 3 (6-mm) red and 3 (11-mm) silver sequins; stuffing; 2 blue wiggle eyes; 12" length red cording; 1 (15-mm) white pom-pom; small package decoration
For the reindeer: copper spray paint, 2 (1¼") squares black felt, 11½" length brown pipe cleaner, 2 brown wiggle eyes, 1 (25-mm) brown pom-pom, 1 small jingle bell, 15" length ¼"-wide red satin ribbon, 12" length silver cording

Note: Silver webbing is found in the spray paint section of stores. You'll find a metric conversion chart on page 5.

Santa
1. On 1 side only, cover 2½" of the shaped end of the paint stick with the masking tape. For each craft stick, tape off 1¼" of 1 end, putting tape on both sides of the stick. **Ask the grown-up** to watch as you spray-paint 1 side each of the paint stick and the craft sticks, using the red paint. Let the paint dry. Paint the remaining sides. Let the paint dry. Spray-paint each side of the

paint stick and the craft sticks with the silver webbing in the same manner. Let the webbing dry. Remove the tape.

2. **Ask the grown-up** to center and drill a hole in the unpainted end of the paint stick near the short edge. Then center and drill a second hole 2½" below the first hole. Center and drill a hole in the painted end of each craft stick near the short edge.

3. Glue 1 (½" x ¾") piece of white felt to each side of each craft stick where the red paint ends and the unpainted area begins (see the illustration). With the unpainted portion of the paint stick facedown, stack the craft sticks on top of the paint stick, aligning all of the holes. Slip the brad through the holes from beneath and bend the prongs. The side the arms are attached to is the back of the ornament.

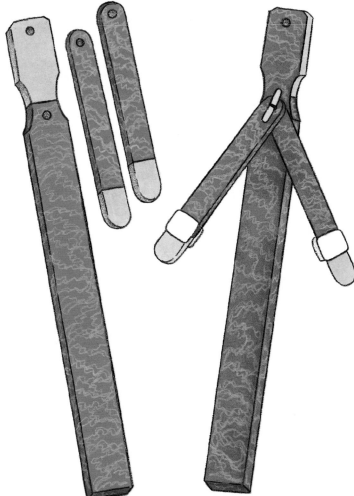

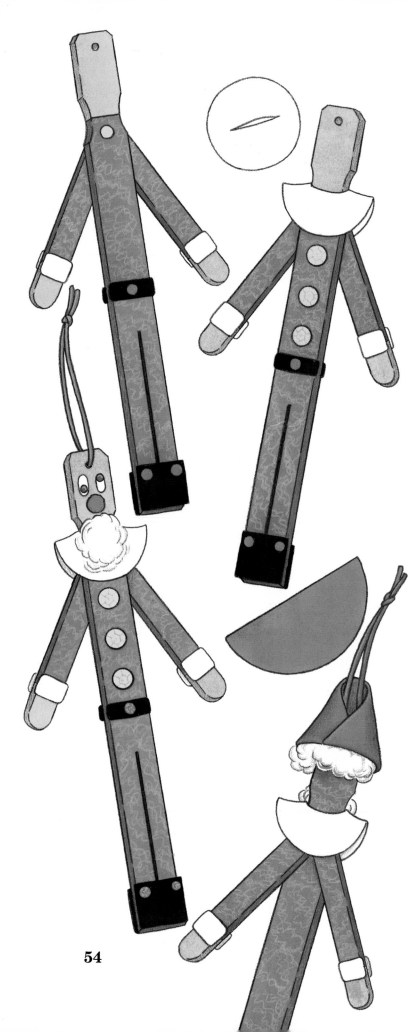

4. For the legs, using the marker and beginning 5¼" from the short painted end of the paint stick, draw a line along the center to the edge (see the illustration). For the boots, glue 1 (1¼") black felt square to each side of the painted end of the paint stick, aligning 1 edge of the square with the short end of the stick. For the belt, glue 1 (¼" x 1⅛") black felt piece to each side of the paint stick, 5" above the top of the boots. Glue 1 red sequin to the center front of the belt and to each top corner of the front of the boots. Let the glue dry.

5. For the collar, cut a slit in the center of the white felt circle. Slip the circle over the unpainted end of the paint stick and slide it to where the craft stick arms begin. Glue the collar in place. Center and glue the 3 silver sequins on the front of the ornament, spacing them evenly between the collar and the belt. Let the glue dry.

6. Referring to the illustration, for the beard, glue a small amount of stuffing to the center front of the collar. Center and glue the red pom-pom nose above the beard. Center and glue the wiggle eyes above the nose. For the hanger, thread the red cording through the hole in the top of the ornament. Align the ends and tie a knot in the cording below the ends. For the hair, glue a ring of stuffing around the end of the paint stick above the eyes. Let the glue dry.

7. Referring to the illustration, for the hat, cut the red circle in half. Using half of the circle, fold the piece around the top of the ornament, overlapping the ends and creating a cone shape. Make sure the hanger extends out of the opening at the top of the hat. Glue the overlapped ends in place. Glue the white pom-pom to the front top of the hat (see the photo). Glue the package to the front of 1 hand. Let the glue dry.

Reindeer

1. **Ask the grown-up** to watch as you spray-paint 1 side of the paint stick, using the copper paint. Let the paint dry. Paint the remaining side. Let the paint dry. Spray-paint each side of the paint stick with the silver webbing in the same manner. Let the webbing dry.

2. **Ask the grown-up** to center and drill a hole in 1 end of the paint stick near the short edge. Center and drill 2 holes side by side ½" below the first hole.

3. For the legs, using the marker and beginning 5¼" from the end without the holes, draw a line along the center of the paint stick to the edge (see the illustration). For the hoofs, glue 1 (1¼") black felt square to both sides of the bottom of the ornament, extending 1 edge of each felt square ¼" off the end of the stick. Cut a notch in the bottom center of the hoofs.

4. Referring to the illustration, for the antlers, cut 1 (6½") length and 2 (2½") lengths from the pipe cleaner. Fold the 6½" length into a U shape. Slip the ends through the 2 drilled holes from beneath; then bend the pipe cleaner prongs up. This is the front of the ornament. Wrap 1 (2½") length of pipe cleaner around each pipe cleaner prong.

5. Referring to the illustration, center and glue the wiggle eyes in place. Center and glue the brown pom-pom in place. Glue the red pom-pom in the center of the brown pom-pom. Thread the jingle bell onto the ribbon. Tie the ribbon into a bow around the ornament below the brown pom-pom.

6. For the hanger, thread the silver cording through the hole in the top of the ornament. Align the ends and tie a knot in the cording below the ends.

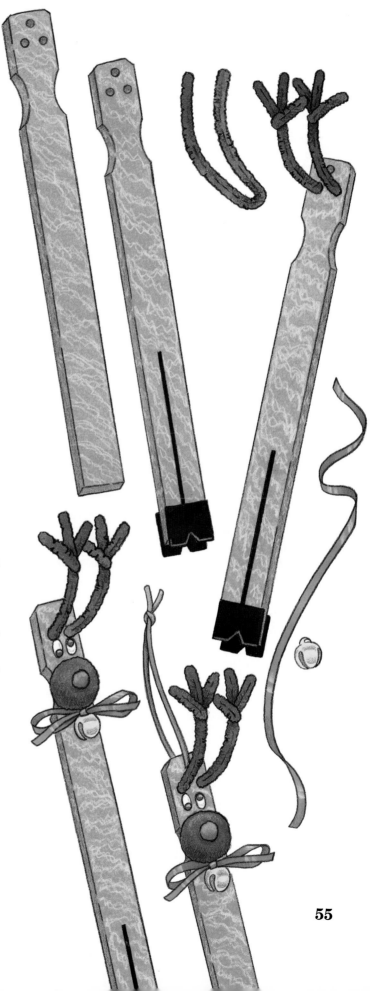

Seeing Stars

Follow our simple recipe for making spice dough stars and then decorate a pot, a package, or a tree with them.

You will need (for the basic Spice Dough Stars):

A grown-up
Large bowl
3 cups all-purpose flour
⅔ cup salt
1⅓ cups water
¼ cup cinnamon
3 tablespoons nutmeg
3 tablespoons ginger
3 tablespoons ground cloves
Dish towel
Baking sheet
Aluminum foil
Waxed paper
Rolling pin
2" metal star cookie cutter
Oven
Gold spray paint
Small paintbrush
Metallic acrylic paint in variety of colors
**For the package toppers and the gar-
land:** coffee stirrer or small straw, twine,
scissors
For the pot: clay flower pot in desired size,
thick craft glue, hard candies or potted
plant (optional)

Note: Dough recipe will make approximately 48 (2") stars. The dough will smell good
once it is mixed, but it should not be eaten.
Never eat the painted stars. You'll find a
metric conversion chart on page 5.

1. In the large bowl, mix the flour, the
salt, and the water until a stiff dough
forms. (You may need to use your hands.)
Add the cinnamon, the nutmeg, the ginger,
and the ground cloves to the dough and
work them in. Roll the dough into a ball.
Put the ball into the bowl. Cover the bowl
loosely with the towel. Refrigerate the covered bowl for 1 hour. (Cold dough is easier
to roll and to cut.)

2. Cover the baking sheet with aluminum
foil. Place a small ball of the dough on a
sheet of waxed paper. Roll the dough out to
½" thickness. Use the cookie cutter to cut
out the star shapes. Place the cutout star
shapes onto the baking sheet. Continue
balling up and rolling out the dough until
there is no more dough. (The more you handle the dough the harder it is to work with.)

**3. For the package toppers and the
garland,** use the coffee stirrer or the straw
to punch a hole in 1 point of each star.

4. Refrigerate all of the stars overnight. The next day, remove the stars from the refrigerator and let them sit and warm to room temperature. **Ask the grown-up** to preheat the oven to 250°. Bake the stars for 1 hour or until they look puffy. Let the stars cool completely.

5. Leave the stars on the aluminum foil and take them outside to spray-paint. **Ask the grown-up** to help you spray-paint 1 side of each star with the gold paint. Let the paint dry. Turn each star over and paint the other side. Let the paint dry.

6. Using the paintbrush and the metallic acrylic paints, paint a colored star on the top of each dough star (see the illustration). Let the paint dry.

7. For the package toppers, cut a length of twine and tie it around your package. Cut another length of twine and thread several stars onto the twine, tying a knot after each star. Tie this twine around the length already on the package.

8. For the garland, cut a length of twine slightly longer than you want the finished garland to be. Thread 1 star onto the twine and slide it to the opposite end. Tie a knot in the twine at the top of the star. Repeat with another star approximately 6" from the first star. Continue in this manner along the entire length of the twine.

9. For the pot, ask the grown-up to help you spray-paint the clay pot with the gold paint. Let the paint dry. Coat the center back of 1 star with thick craft glue. Stick the star onto the outside of the pot. Continue gluing stars to the pot as desired. Let the glue dry. If desired, fill several small pots with individually wrapped hard candies or fill a large pot with a potted plant.

Surprise Balls

It's a present! No, it's an ornament. Actually, it's both! Simply find the plastic ornaments at your craft store—they come in all shapes and sizes. Then fill them with colorful surprises.

You will need:
Plastic ball ornaments that open
Golf tees, embroidery floss, jacks and ball, or other small gifts
Paper curling ribbon: red, green, gold

1. Decide who you want to give an ornament gift to and then choose a colorful surprise. The balls shown here are filled with tees for a golfer, embroidery floss for a stitcher, and jacks for a young friend. There are lots of other possibilities, so use your imagination and have fun!

2. Cut a 12″ piece each of red, green, and gold ribbon. Thread the ribbons through the opening at the top of the ornament and tie them in a knot. Carefully pull the edge of scissors across the ribbon to make it curl.

Level 1

Just Ducky!

There's nothing daffy about these ducks! Dressed for the holidays in their best top hats, they'll make dandy decorations for your Christmas tree.

You will need (for each):
Tracing paper
Pencil
Scissors
Blue, white, and yellow felt
2 small white powder puffs
White glue
Sequins
Rickrack
Scrap of fabric (for the scarf)
Ribbon

1. Trace the patterns for the duck's hat, tail, bill, and foot on tracing paper. Cut out the patterns. Draw around the hat on blue felt, the tail on white felt, and the bill and foot on yellow felt. Cut out the felt pieces.

2. Glue the edge of one powder puff over the edge of the other powder puff to make the duck's head and body. Let the glue dry.

3. Glue the bill, foot, and tail to the underside of the duck.

4. On the front of the duck, glue a sequin for the eye. Glue rickrack on the hat and then glue sequins on the rickrack. Glue the hat onto the duck's head.

5. Cut a strip from the scrap of fabric for the scarf. Tie it around the duck's neck. Glue the scarf to keep it in place.

6. For a hanger, glue the ends of the ribbon to the back of the hat.

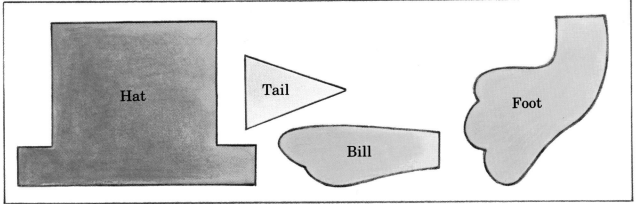

Hat

Tail

Bill

Foot

Christmas Tree Skirt

Wrap some felt rectangles with ribbons and glue them to this easy-to-make green felt tree skirt. That way you'll always be sure to find packages under your Christmas tree even if Santa hasn't made his visit yet.

You will need:
Pencil or marker
Pushpin
36" of string
2 yards (72"-wide) green felt
Scissors
7½ yards of white giant rickrack
Fabric glue
Felt rectangles: 8 colors (for white and
    yellow, use double layers so the green
    felt doesn't show through)
Variety of ribbons
Liquid ravel preventer
Twist ties
Ruler

1. To make a compass, tie the pencil to 1 end of the string and the pushpin to the other end. Stick the pushpin in the center of the felt. With the string and pencil, draw a large circle. Cut the string to 5" and make a smaller circle in the center of the large circle. Cut out the large circle. Cut straight up from the edge of the large circle to the small circle and then cut out the small circle to make an opening for the tree trunk.

2. With fabric glue, glue the rickrack to the inner and outer edges of the circle. Apply liquid ravel preventer to the ends of the rickrack to keep the ends from fraying.

3. To make the packages, choose ribbons to coordinate with each felt rectangle. Measure across the width, or down the length, or even diagonally across a corner of the felt. Cut the ribbon that length. Apply liquid ravel preventer to the ribbon ends so they won't fray. Let the ends dry. Then glue the ribbon to the felt. With the twist ties and the same ribbon or another coordinating ribbon, make a bow to add to the top of the package. Glue the bow in place. Decorate all the felt rectangles with ribbons.

4. Place the packages around the skirt, about 7½″ from the outer edge. Once you have all the packages arranged the way you want, glue them in place. Let the glue dry.

Glittery Snowflakes

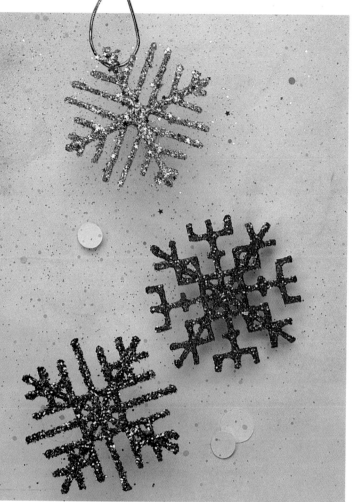

Note: You'll find a metric conversion chart on page 5.

1. Cut the bottom out of the plastic berry basket. Trim this bottom piece to the desired snowflake shape.

2. Place the plastic snowflake on a sheet of waxed paper. Coat 1 side of the snowflake with the glue. Sprinkle glitter on top of the glue. Place the snowflake on the bottom half of the open egg carton. Let the glue dry. Repeat to apply glitter to the other side of the snowflake.

3. For the hanger, tie the gold thread or cord around 1 prong of the snowflake. Tie the ends of the thread together in a knot.

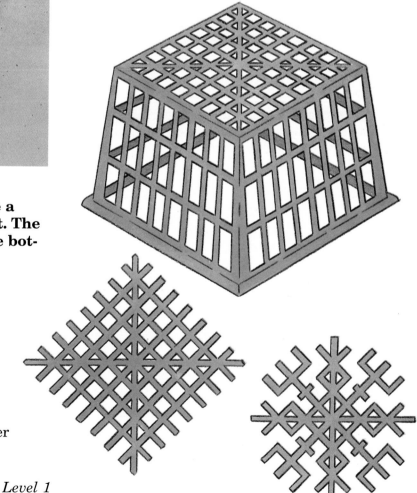

These sparkly ornaments are a quick-and-easy recycling project. The snowflake base is made from the bottom of a plastic berry basket.

You will need (for 1 snowflake ornament):
Plastic berry basket
Scissors
Waxed paper
Craft glue
Glitter in desired color
Foam egg carton
6" gold thread or gold cord for hanger

Level 1

Oodles  of Noodles

Macaroni comes in lots of shapes and sizes. The shapes used for these ornaments are wagon wheels and small and large bow ties. But when the macaroni is glued and painted, it'll be hard to tell they were once just oodles of noodles.

Tree

You will need:
A grown-up
Waxed paper
Founder's Adhesive glue
11 wagon wheel macaronis
Green spray paint
10 small red decorative balls
6" of gold thread

1. Cover your work surface with waxed paper. To form the tree, glue the wagon wheels together in rows as follows. Row 1 has only 1 wheel. Glue 2 wheels together for Row 2. Glue 3 wheels together for Row 3. Glue 4 wheels together for Row 4. Then glue the 4 rows together as shown. For the tree trunk, glue 1 wheel at the center of the bottom row. Let the glue dry.

2. Ask the grown-up to help you spray-paint both sides of the tree. Be sure to do this outside or in a well-ventilated room. Let the paint dry.

3. Glue the red balls in the center of each wheel on rows 1–4.

4. To make a hanger, slip the gold thread through the top opening in the top wheel and knot the ends of the thread.

67

Bow Tie Wreath

You will need:
A grown-up
Waxed paper
Founder's Adhesive glue
7 bow tie macaroni
4 small egg bow macaroni
Spray paints: green, red
Gold glitter paint
6" of gold thread

1. Cover your work surface with waxed paper. Glue 6 bow tie macaronis together in a circle, slightly overlapping their edges. Let them dry.

2. Ask the grown-up to help you spray-paint the wreath green. Let it dry. For the bows, spray-paint the remaining bow tie and 4 small egg bow macaronis red. Let them dry.

3. Glue the large red bow to the top of the wreath, overlapping 2 green macaronis as shown.

4. Glue the small red bows to the center of the remaining green bows.

5. Dot the center of the red bows with glitter paint.

6. For a hanger, fold the gold thread in half and glue the ends to the top back of the wreath.

68

Spoon Angel

3. Tear off a small clump of yellow shred and glue it to the back of the spoon over the ends of the hanger. Hold the shred in place until it sticks. Let the glue dry.

4. Bend the star garland to make a circle and twist the ends together. Slip the garland over the hanger loop and onto the top of the head.

5. Using the markers, draw a face.

For a holiday giggle, decorate your tree with this impish angel. A silly smile, fanciful hair, and a tilted halo transform an ordinary plastic spoon into a whimsical Christmas ornament.

You will need:
10" length 3"-wide foil craft ribbon
White plastic spoon
Scissors
12" length of fishing line
Cellophane tape
Yellow shred
Glue
5" length of multicolored star garland
Fine-point permanent markers: black, red

1. Tie the ribbon around the spoon handle. Trim and shape the ribbon ends.

2. For the hanger, fold the fishing line in half and knot the ends together. Tape the ends to the back of the spoon.

Level 1   **69**

Ribbon Candy

They may look good enough to eat, but these ribbon candies are strictly treats for the tree. Collect scraps of striped ribbon or find ribbons in Christmas colors to make a wide assortment of "flavors."

You will need:

A grown-up
Waxed paper
Liquid fabric stiffener
Paintbrush
Craft ribbons: 12" (⅝"- to
   ¾"-wide) lengths,
   24" (1½"-wide) lengths
Rustproof, fine straight pins
Flat piece of Styrofoam
Pliers (optional)
Scissors
Sharp needle
Silver thread

1. Cover your work space with waxed paper.

2. Follow the directions on the fabric stiffener bottle and paint the stiffener on both sides of 1 piece of ribbon. Smooth the stiffener with the paintbrush for an even coat.

3. Stick a pin into the Styrofoam through the center of the ribbon. Form tight curls in the ribbon and hold them in place with straight pins. Try to keep all the curls the same height, about ¾" high for narrow ribbons and 1" high for wide ribbons.

4. Leave the pins in place but lightly pull the ribbon away from the Styrofoam so that the ribbon doesn't stick to the Styrofoam when the stiffener dries.

5. Let the ribbon dry thoroughly. **Ask the grown-up** to remove the pins from the ribbon, using the pliers if desired.

6. Cut 1 end of the ribbon curl into a point. To make a hanger, insert a 10" length of thread through the tip of the point. Tie the ends of the thread together.

71

Nutty Reindeer Ornaments

Oh, nuts! That's about all it takes to make these nutty reindeer. This herd includes a peanut, a walnut, a Brazil nut, an almond, and a hazelnut. Create your own mixed herd or choose your favorite nut and make a matching family.

You will need (for each):
A grown-up
Nut
Nutcracker
Pen
Tracing paper
Scissors
Green construction paper
Red felt
Tacky glue
10" piece of red cord or ribbon
Toothpick
2 (7-mm) wiggle eyes
1 small red pom-pom

1. **Ask the grown-up** to help you crack the nut in half. Remove the meat from the shell. Choose the best-shaped shell half and set the other half aside.

2. Trace and cut out the antler pattern. Cut 1 pair of antlers from the green construction paper.

3. For the ornament back, place the shell on the red felt and trace around it. Cut out the felt.

4. Glue the antlers to the back of the top or wider end of the nut. For the hanger, fold the cord in half and glue the 2 ends to the back of the antlers. Then glue the red felt to the back, covering the cord and the back of the antlers.

5. Squeeze a little glue onto the toothpick. Dab the glue on the back of the wiggle eyes. Glue the eyes in place. Glue on the red pom-pom nose. Let the ornament dry.

Antlers

Animal Zoobilee

Blue-striped zebras and purple polka-dotted giraffes! These wonderful wild animals are ready for your holiday jubilee. Tie one to a package or use a bunch to brighten a wreath or tree.

You will need (for each animal):
Tracing paper
Pencil
Scissors
Fun Foam in assorted colors
Tacky glue
2 (3-mm) wiggle eyes
Needle
Monofilament thread

1. Trace and cut out the desired animal pattern.

2. Lay the pattern on the foam and trace around it.

3. Trace the other animal details on a contrasting color of foam. For the elephant, trace and cut out 2 ears. for the lion, trace and cut 2 manes and 1 face. Clip the edges of the manes to make the fringe.

Details for the other animals don't need patterns. Cut out stripes for the front and back of the zebra. Cut 6 tiny triangles for the alligator teeth. For the giraffe, cut out circles in various sizes and colors.

4. Glue 1 ear to each side of the elephant. Glue the lion's face to 1 mane. Glue the face/mane to 1 side of the body and the second mane to the other side of the body. Glue the stripes to both sides of the zebra. Glue 3 teeth to both sides of the alligator. Glue the circles to both sides of the giraffe.

5. Glue wiggle eyes on both sides of all the animals except the lion. (He's facing forward.)

6. For each hanger, cut a 10″ piece of monofilament thread. Thread the needle and run it through the top center of the animal. Tie the ends of the thread in a knot.

Alligator

76

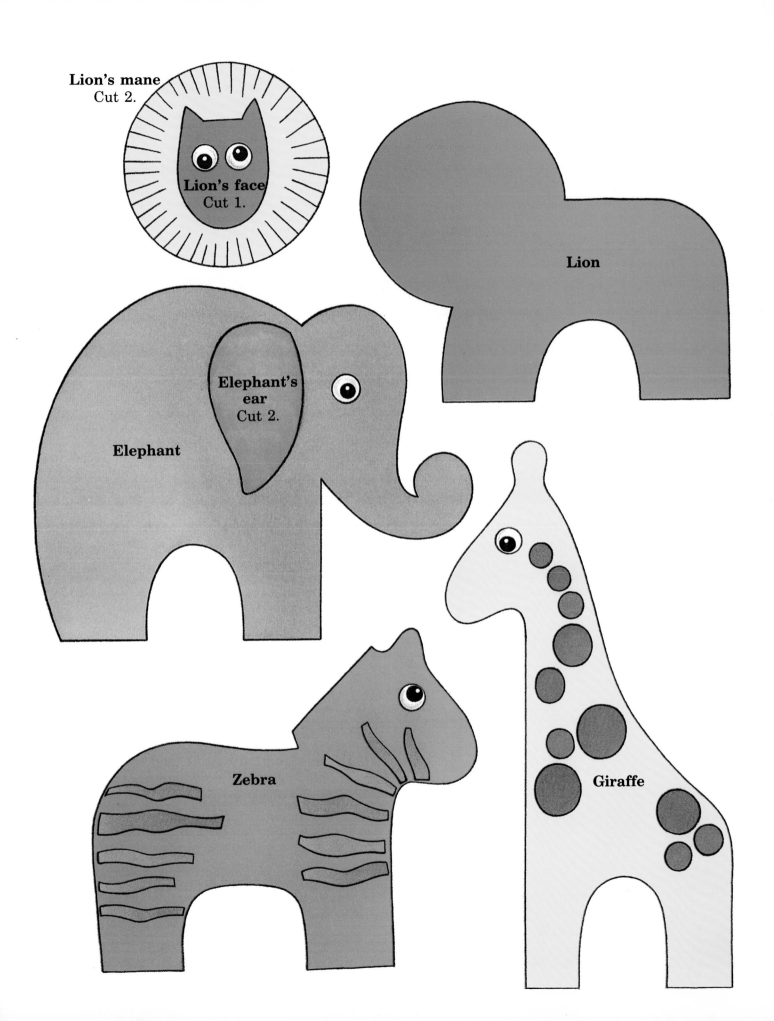

Lion's mane
Cut 2.

Lion's face
Cut 1.

Lion

Elephant's ear
Cut 2.

Elephant

Zebra

Giraffe

Glitter Ornaments

Glue plus glitter
equals a golden holiday.
When light hits the tiny particles of
gold on these ornaments, your tree
will sparkle from every branch.

Glitter Sticks

You will need (for 1 ornament):
Waxed paper
8″ of gold thread
Glue
Wooden craft stick
Paintbrush
Gold glitter

1. Cover your work surface with waxed
paper.

2. To make the hanger, fold the thread
in half and glue the ends to the craft
stick. Let the glue dry.

3. Using the paintbrush, spread 1 side of
the craft stick with glue. Sprinkle glitter
over the glue. Let the glue dry. Then
spread glue and sprinkle glitter on the
other side of the stick.

Star Brights

You will need (for 1 ornament):
Waxed paper
Brass screw eye
1 (1½"-diameter) Styrofoam ball
Glue
50 wooden toothpicks
Gold glitter
8" of gold thread

1. Cover your work surface with waxed paper.

2. Push the screw eye into the center top of the ball.

3. Squeeze some glue on the waxed paper. Roll each toothpick in the glue. Place the toothpicks on the waxed paper and sprinkle them with glitter. Turn the toothpicks over and sprinkle them again. Let them dry.

4. Push each toothpick into the ball, using the diagram as a guide.

5. To make the hanger, slip the gold thread through the screw eye and knot the ends together.

79

Sticky-Star Balls

You will need (for 1 ornament):
Waxed paper
Brass screw eye
1 (2½"- to 4"-diameter) Styrofoam ball
Toothpick
Glue
Gold glitter
Gold self-adhesive stars
12" (½"-wide) gold ribbon
8" length gold thread

1. Cover your work surface with waxed paper.

2. Push the screw eye into the center top of the ball.

3. Using the toothpick, spread some glue onto the ball. Sprinkle the ball with glitter and let it dry.

4. Decorate the ball as desired with the star stickers. (If the stars don't stick to the ball, glue them in place.)

5. Thread half of the ribbon through the screw eye and tie it in a bow.

6. To make the hanger, slip the gold thread through the screw eye and knot the ends together.

Paper Plate Angel

Snip, shape, and tape paper plates to make this angel. She'll look so pretty at the top of your tree!

You will need:
Pencil
Tracing paper
Scissors
2 (9"-diameter) paper plates
Yellow construction paper
Glue stick
Black and red fine-tip markers
Clear tape

1. Trace and cut out the patterns.

2. Draw around the wing pattern on one of the paper plates as shown. Turn the pattern over and draw around it again. Cut out the wings.

3. Turn the other plate bottom side up. Place the angel pattern on the plate as shown and draw around the top edge of the pattern. Cut out the angel. Then cut along the broken lines.

4. Use the markers to draw the angel's eyes and mouth. Cut out a halo from the yellow construction paper and glue it to the back of the angel's head. Let dry.

5. Tape the edges of the angel's skirt together. Put the wings in the slits. Use tape to hold the wings in place. Glue the angel's hands together and let dry.

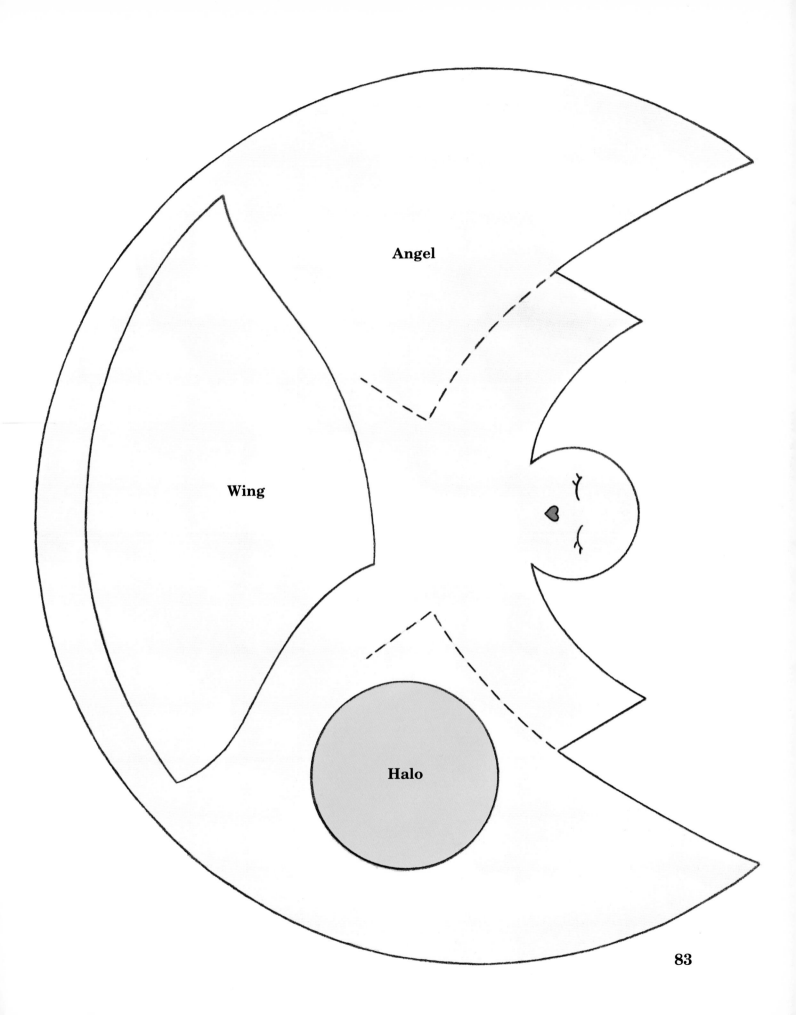

Angel

Wing

Halo

83

Window Wonderland

Use tissue paper cutouts to make a stained-glass window. Watch it glow when the sun shines through.

You will need:
Colored markers
Tissue paper
Scissors
Clear self-stick paper
Hole punch
Curling ribbon
Clear tape

1. Using the markers, draw holiday pictures on the tissue paper.

2. Cut out the pictures, leaving a border of tissue paper around each one.

3. Cut two pieces of self-stick paper big enough to cover each picture. Lay one piece of self-stick paper, sticky side up, on the table. Put the picture on top and cover it with the second piece of self-stick paper. Cut out the picture, following the outline.

4. Punch a hole in the top of each ornament. Pull a piece of ribbon through the hole and tie the ends to make a loop for hanging. Curl the ribbon ends.

5. Use tape to hang the ornaments in a window.

Peppermint Ponies

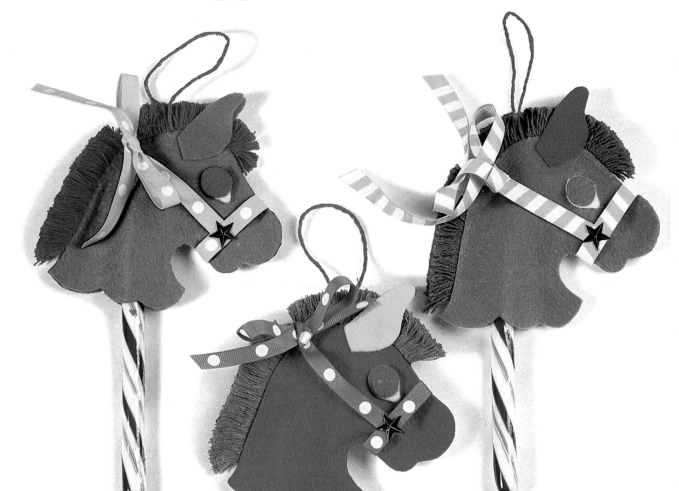

Turn plain-Jane candy canes into holiday hobbyhorses. Hitch them to your tree or to presents for friends.

You will need (for each pony):
Pencil
Tracing paper
Scissors
2 (5") squares of felt for the head
Scraps of felt for the eye and ear
5½" piece of fringe
Tacky craft glue
String
25½" length ribbon
Paper clips (for holding glued pieces while they dry)
Star sequin
Candy cane

1. Trace and cut out the patterns.

2. Pin the head pattern to two layers of felt and cut out the heads. Cut a felt ear, eye, and pupil.

3. Cut away the loops on the fringe. Glue the fringe to the edge of one head. Cut a piece of string for a hanger and glue the ends to the top of the head.

4. Glue the edges of the second head to the first head, leaving the bottom edges open. Glue the ear and eye in place.

5. To make a halter, cut a 4½″ piece of ribbon. Wrap the ribbon around the horse's muzzle. Overlap the ends and glue them together. Cut the remaining ribbon in half. Glue one end of each ribbon to the underside of the muzzle ribbon. Glue a sequin to the halter. Let the glue dry.

6. Tie the loose ribbon ends into a bow. Gently slip the curved end of the candy cane into the cover, aiming the tip towards the horse's muzzle.

Head

Ear

Pupil

Eye

87

Cookie-Cutter Kids

Cinnamon and applesauce make these cookie look-alikes smell as sweet as they look.

You will need:
3¾-ounce can of cinnamon plus extra
  for dusting
Applesauce
Large bowl
Tablespoon and mixing spoon
Waxed paper
Rolling pin and spatula
Small gingerbread-man cookie cutter
Toothpick and emery board
Slick pens
Buttons, beads, fabric scraps, rickrack,
  and other trim
White glue
Ribbon for hangers

1. Pour the can of cinnamon into the bowl. Add several tablespoons of applesauce and blend with the mixing spoon. Keep adding applesauce, a tablespoon at a time, to make a thick dough. Shape the dough into a ball.

2. Lightly dust a piece of waxed paper and the rolling pin with cinnamon. Place the ball of dough in the center of the paper. Flatten the ball with your hand and then roll it ¼" thick.

3. Using the cookie cutter, cut out the kids. Dust the spatula with cinnamon. Gently lift the kids and place them on a clean piece of waxed paper.

4. Use the toothpick to make a hole in the top of each kid. Let the kids dry for at least 24 hours, turning them often.

5. When the kids are thoroughly dry, sand any rough edges with the emery board. Decorate the kids and let dry.

6. Use ribbon for hangers.

Jumping Jack

Oh, how jolly this elf will be, dancing on your Christmas tree!

You will need:
Pencil
Tracing paper
Poster paper
Felt-tip markers
Scissors
Hole punch
8 small brads
Ribbon

1. Trace the patterns, pressing hard with your pencil.

2. Turn the tracings over and retrace them onto poster paper. Color the pieces.

3. Cut out the pieces. Punch a hole through each X. Assemble the pieces, using the brads.

4. Tie a ribbon around the jumping jack's cap and make a bow. Tie another ribbon to the cap ribbon for a hanger.

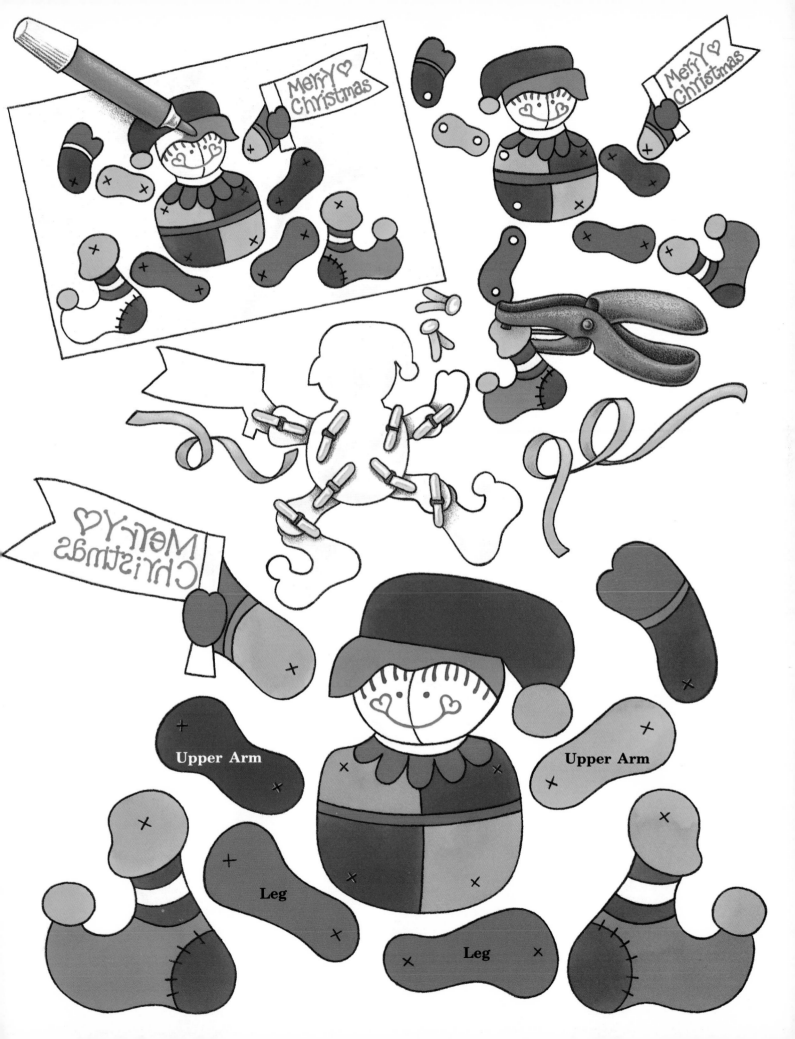

Merry ♥ Christmas

Merry ♥ Christmas

Merry ♥ Christmas

Upper Arm

Upper Arm

Leg

Leg

For the Mantel

Away in a Manger

Setting up a scene that looks like the stable where Jesus was born is a nice way to celebrate Christmas. You can make Mary and Joseph, Baby Jesus, the shepherds and kings, an angel, and the animals for the scene, which is called a crèche, from felt. Glue the felt figures onto blocks of wood. Place them on a mantel or a table or under the Christmas tree.

Before you start: Ask your mom or dad to cut six (7½"-long) blocks, four (6"-long) blocks, and three (4"-long) blocks from a 2" x 4" x 8' pine stud. After the blocks are cut, rub sandpaper on the ends to make them smooth.

You will need:
12 envelopes
Pencil
Tracing paper
Scissors
Different colors of felt
13 blocks of wood
White glue
Ribbon, braid, rickrack
Sequins
Felt-tip marker

1. Look at the picture of the crèche figures and read the labels on the pattern pieces to see which pattern pieces go with each figure. Notice that sometimes you use the same pattern pieces to make different figures.

2. Label the envelopes with the names of the different figures. Trace the pattern pieces for each figure onto tracing paper. Cut out the pattern pieces. Put them in the envelope that is labeled with the figure's name.

3. Working on one figure at a time, draw around the pattern pieces on different colors of felt. Notice that you will need to turn over the pattern pieces for Mary and the Second Shepherd before you draw around them so that the figures will face in different directions.

4. Cut out the felt pieces for one figure at a time. As you finish cutting out each figure, put the felt pieces in place on a block that is the right size. (Put Baby Jesus and the Lambs on the 4″ blocks; put Mary, the Third King, the Donkey, and the Cow on the 6″ blocks; and put Joseph, the Angel, the First King, the Second King, the First Shepherd, and the Second Shepherd on the 7½″ blocks.)

5. When you have finished cutting out the pieces for the figures and have put them in place, glue them onto the blocks.

6. Glue bits of ribbon, braid, and rickrack onto the figures for trim. Glue sequins on the kings. Cut "spots" from felt and glue them on the cow. Make features for the figures' faces with the felt-tip marker or tiny pieces of felt.

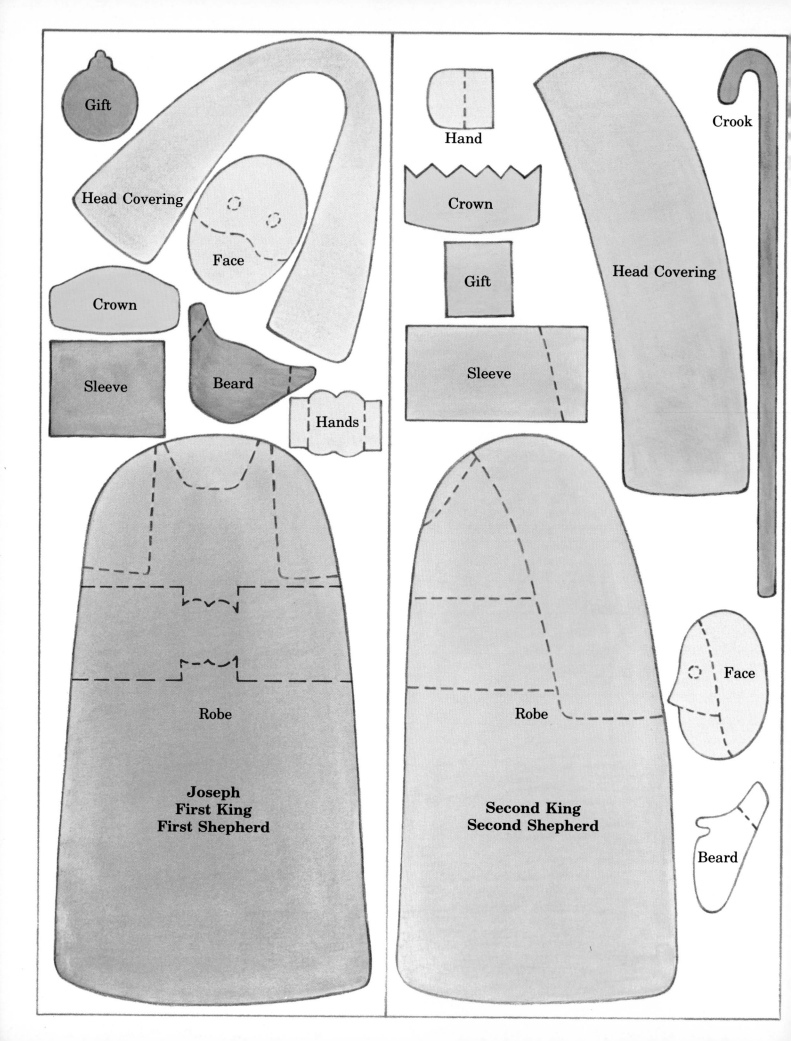

Gift

Head Covering

Face

Crown

Sleeve

Beard

Hands

Robe

**Joseph
First King
First Shepherd**

Hand

Crown

Gift

Sleeve

Head Covering

Crook

Robe

Face

Beard

**Second King
Second Shepherd**

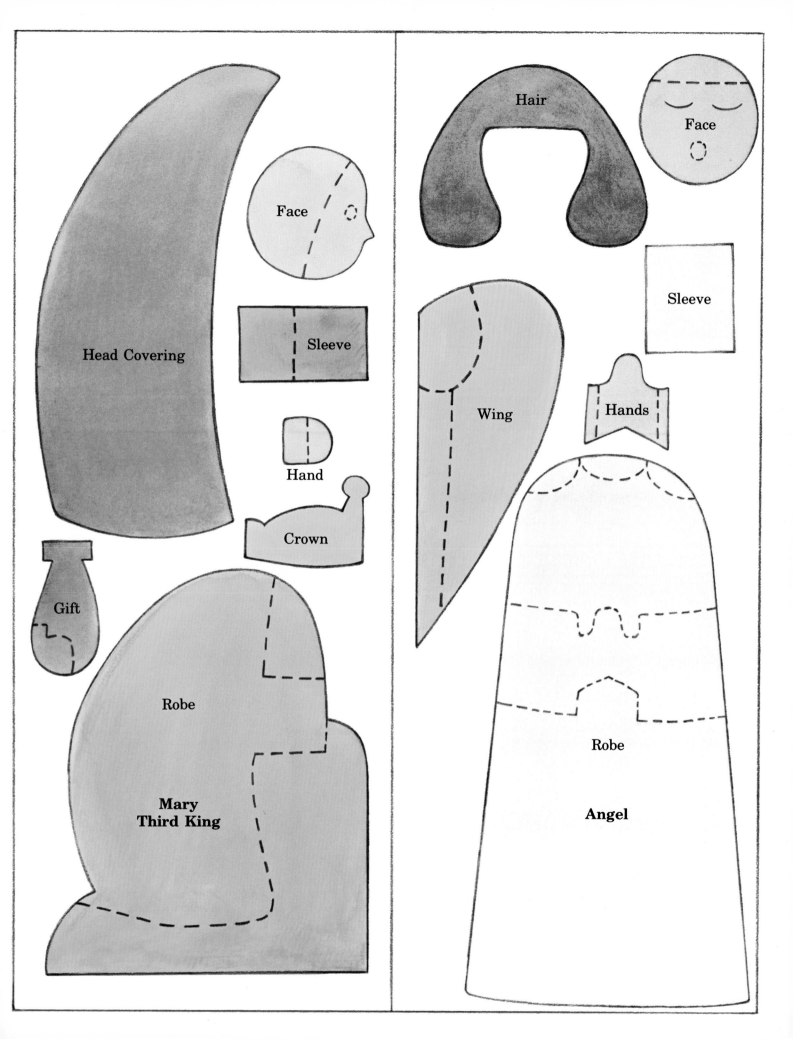

Face

Head Covering

Sleeve

Hand

Crown

Gift

Robe

**Mary
Third King**

Hair

Face

Sleeve

Wing

Hands

Robe

Angel

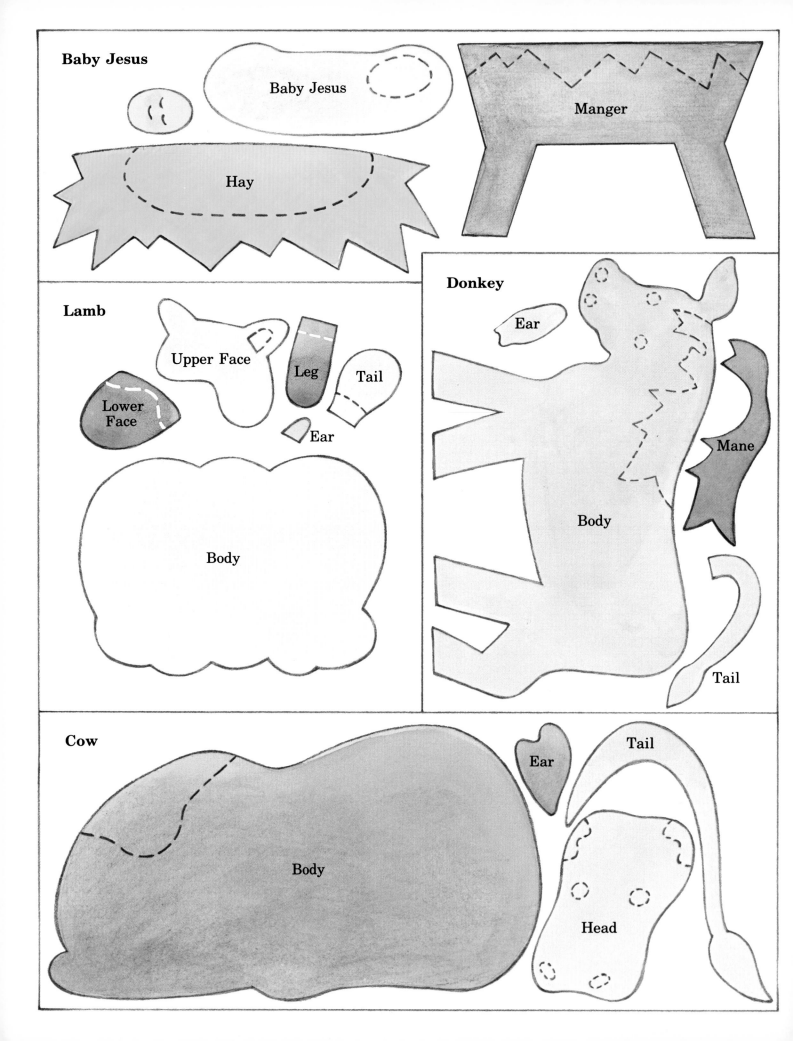

Pop Goes the Snowman

Make this frosty figure for a centerpiece that won't melt when the sun comes out. Simply cover balloons with glue-coated string, let them dry, and pop the balloons to leave airy "snowballs."

You will need:

3 balloons
16 ounces of white glue
Medium-size plastic bowl
250 yards of white string
Tweezers
1 (20″-diameter) white Styrofoam ring
Scrap of orange ribbon
Scrap of black felt
Scissors
Small black felt hat
3 large black beads
2¼″ x 27″ piece of red-and-white stripe
   fabric for scarf
Liquid ravel preventer

Note: Our model is 21″ tall, but you can make your snowman smaller or larger by adjusting the sizes of the balloons.

1. Blow up 1 balloon each for the head, the middle, and the bottom of the snowman, varying the sizes as shown.

2. Pour the glue into the plastic bowl and dip the string into the glue. Remove the excess glue with your fingers.

3. For each balloon: Wrap the string around the balloon until you have formed a thick webbing and then cut the string. Let the balloon dry for several hours. Pop the balloon and carefully remove the deflated material using the tweezers.

4. Glue the head, the middle, and the bottom together to form the body. Glue the bottom of the snowman in the center of the Styrofoam ring. Let the glue dry.

5. To make the nose, roll the orange ribbon into a cone shape and glue the ends together. Glue the nose in the center of the top balloon.

6. From the black felt, cut out 2 large circles for the eyes and 6 small circles for the mouth. Glue the eyes and the mouth in place on the top balloon. Glue the hat onto the top of the snowman's head.

7. Glue the beads in a straight line down the center of the middle balloon.

8. Apply a light coat of liquid ravel preventer to the long edges of the red-and-white stripe strip. To make fringe, cut tiny slits in each short edge. Wrap the scarf around the snowman's neck and tie it in place.

Fun Foam Forest

You won't need a ladder to trim these trees! And you can choose all the decorations yourself. Make one tree or a whole forest for a festive Christmas centerpiece.

You will need (for each tree):
Tracing paper
Pencil
Scissors
Fun Foam: green, yellow, blue, black, red, orange, white
Founder's Adhesive glue
Water-soluble marker
Ruler
Hole punch (optional)
For the teardrop lights tree: fine-point permanent black marker

1. Decide which size tree you want to make—small, medium, or large. Trace and cut out the desired tree and star patterns. Trace the patterns 2 times onto the color foam indicated. Cut them out, making sure to mark the bottom center on each triangle.

2. To make the star, glue the 2 pieces together along the outside edges, leaving the bottom unglued. Set the star aside.

3. Using the water-soluble marker and the ruler, draw a straight line from the peak of the tree to the bottom center on 1 side of each triangle. Mark the center point of the tree on each line. On 1 triangle, cut along the marked line from the peak to the center point. On the other triangle, cut along the marked line from the bottom to the center point.

4. Referring to the photo, cut the decorations from assorted colors of foam and glue them to the triangles as desired. (Use the hole punch to make small circles.) **For the teardrop lights tree:** Referring to the photo and using the marker, draw scalloped lines on the front and the back of each triangle. Glue 1 teardrop at the tip of each scallop. Let the glue dry.

5. To form the tree, slide the triangle with the slit at the bottom into the triangle with the slit at the top. Place the star on top of the tree so that the top edges of the tree fit inside.

Large Star
Cut 2.

104

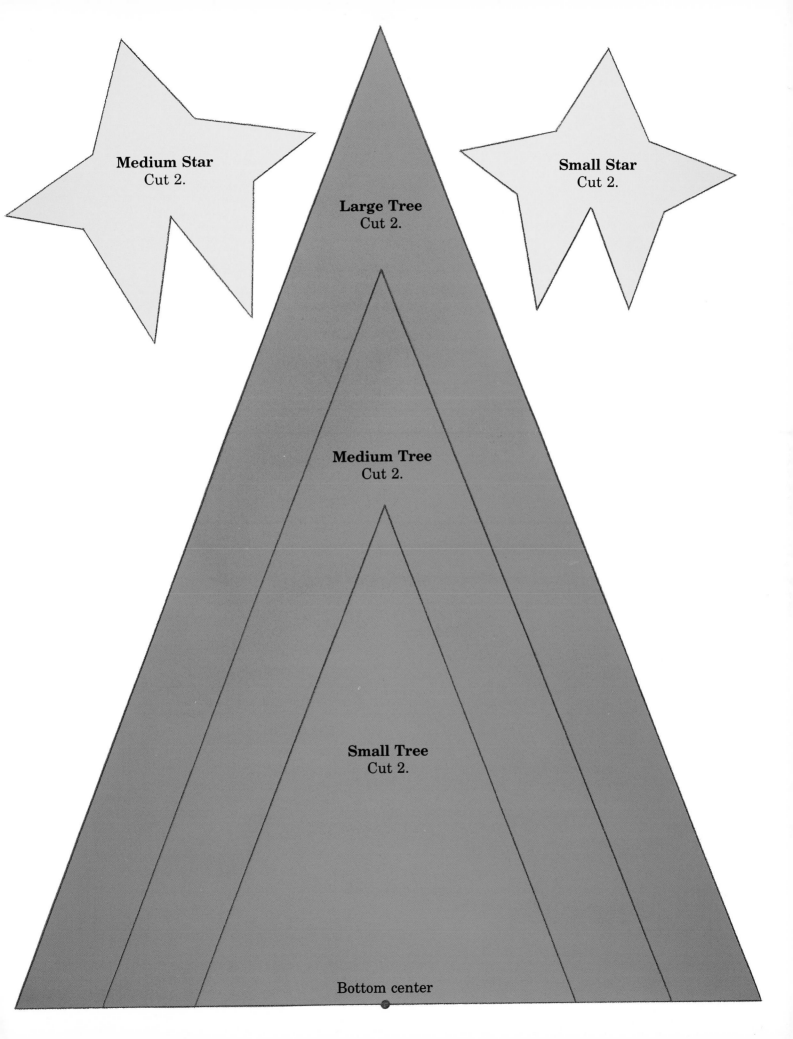

Medium Star
Cut 2.

Small Star
Cut 2.

Large Tree
Cut 2.

Medium Tree
Cut 2.

Small Tree
Cut 2.

Bottom center

Sugarplum Trees

These topiaries will brighten up any tabletop or desk. We used candy circles, but many candies would work.

You will need (for 2 topiaries):
A grown-up
2 (4"-diameter) clay pots
2 (12") lengths ⁵⁄₁₆"-diameter wooden dowels
Acrylic paints: white, red, green, blue, yellow
Paintbrushes
Spray varnish
Tracing paper
Pencil
Scissors
10" square cardboard
Craft knife
Paper plate
10" x 16" x 1" piece white Styrofoam
Serrated kitchen knife
Waxed paper
Founder's Adhesive glue
Candy circles in variety of colors
Florist's clay
Pebbles
1 (26") length each grosgrain ribbon: red with white polka dots, blue with white polka dots

Note: The candy that is glued to the Styrofoam shapes is **not** to be eaten.

1. Paint the pots and the dowels white. Let the paint dry. Paint alternating red and green curvy stripes on 1 pot, including the rim. Let the paint dry. **Ask the grown-up** to spray the pot with the varnish.

2. Paint blue curvy stripes on the remaining pot, ending the stripes at the rim. Let the paint dry. Trace the small star pattern onto the tracing paper. Cut it out. Transfer the star pattern onto the cardboard scrap. **Ask the grown-up** to cut it out, using the craft knife.

3. Pour a small amount of yellow paint onto the paper plate. Dip the cardboard star into the paint. Referring to the photo, stamp the small star shape around the rim of the pot with the blue stripes. Let the paint dry. **Ask the grown-up** to spray the pot with the varnish.

4. Trace the large star and tree patterns onto the tracing paper. Using the pencil, transfer the shapes onto the Styrofoam. **Ask the grown-up** to cut out the shapes, using the kitchen knife.

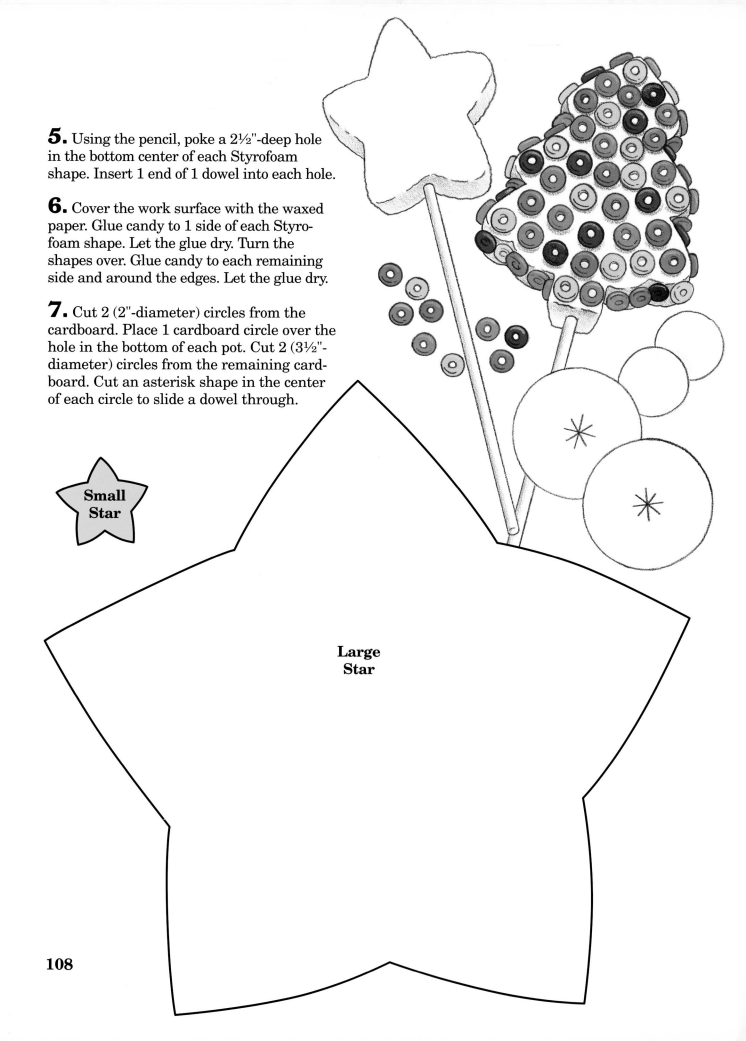

5. Using the pencil, poke a 2½"-deep hole in the bottom center of each Styrofoam shape. Insert 1 end of 1 dowel into each hole.

6. Cover the work surface with the waxed paper. Glue candy to 1 side of each Styrofoam shape. Let the glue dry. Turn the shapes over. Glue candy to each remaining side and around the edges. Let the glue dry.

7. Cut 2 (2"-diameter) circles from the cardboard. Place 1 cardboard circle over the hole in the bottom of each pot. Cut 2 (3½"-diameter) circles from the remaining cardboard. Cut an asterisk shape in the center of each circle to slide a dowel through.

Small Star

Large Star

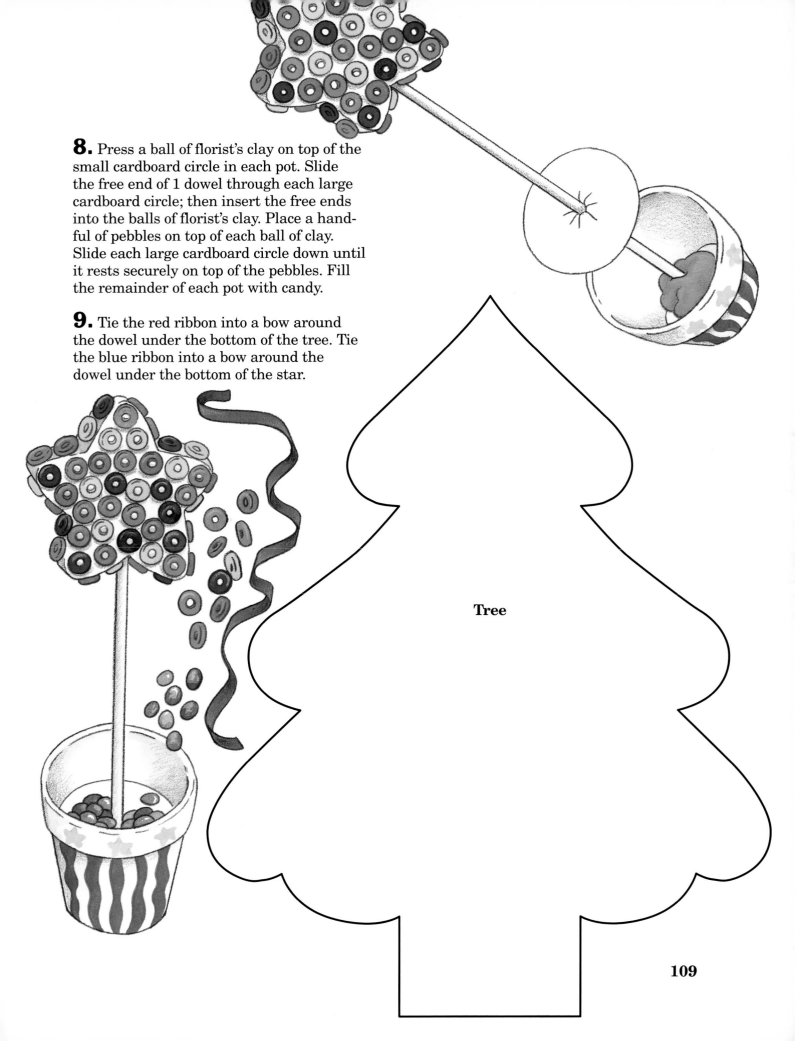

8. Press a ball of florist's clay on top of the small cardboard circle in each pot. Slide the free end of 1 dowel through each large cardboard circle; then insert the free ends into the balls of florist's clay. Place a handful of pebbles on top of each ball of clay. Slide each large cardboard circle down until it rests securely on top of the pebbles. Fill the remainder of each pot with candy.

9. Tie the red ribbon into a bow around the dowel under the bottom of the tree. Tie the blue ribbon into a bow around the dowel under the bottom of the star.

Tree

109

Pet Stockings

Include a furry friend in your celebration with a clever stocking. Then stuff it with surprises that come in small sizes!

You will need (for each stocking):
Tracing paper
Pencil
Scissors
Water-soluble marker
Fabric glue
1⅛ yards of yellow yarn
Large-eyed needle
¾ yard of thin pink paper cording
For the bone: ¼ yard of orange felt; scraps of red, yellow, pink, and green felt; ¾ yard 1"-wide green polka-dot ribbon
For the mouse: ¼ yard of red felt, scraps of pink and blue felt, ⅝ yard ⅛"-wide blue satin ribbon, ¾ yard 1"-wide blue polka-dot ribbon

1. Trace and cut out the desired stocking pattern, marking the stitching lines. Trace the pattern onto the felt 2 times. Cut out the pieces. Using the water-soluble marker, transfer the stitching lines to 1 stocking piece. **For the mouse:** Also transfer stitching lines to each leg piece.

Trace and cut out the details. Trace the details onto the color of felt indicated and cut them out. Set the details aside.

2. For the mouse: Glue the feet to 1 side of the unmarked stocking piece (see the pattern for placement). Cut small slits in the feet to make the toes. Referring to the photo, glue the outside edge of each leg to the remaining stocking piece, aligning the marked stitching lines. Let the glue dry. Thread the needle with the yarn and knot 1 end. Using the yellow yarn and a running stitch, sew each leg to the stocking front along the **inside edge only**. Then stitch the 2 center stitches to finish the legs (see the photo). Knot the thread to secure and cut it off.

3. Place the stocking front faceup on the stocking back, aligning the edges. Thread the needle with the yarn and knot 1 end. Using the yellow yarn and a running stitch, sew the stocking pieces together, following the marked stitching lines. Knot the thread to secure and cut it off.

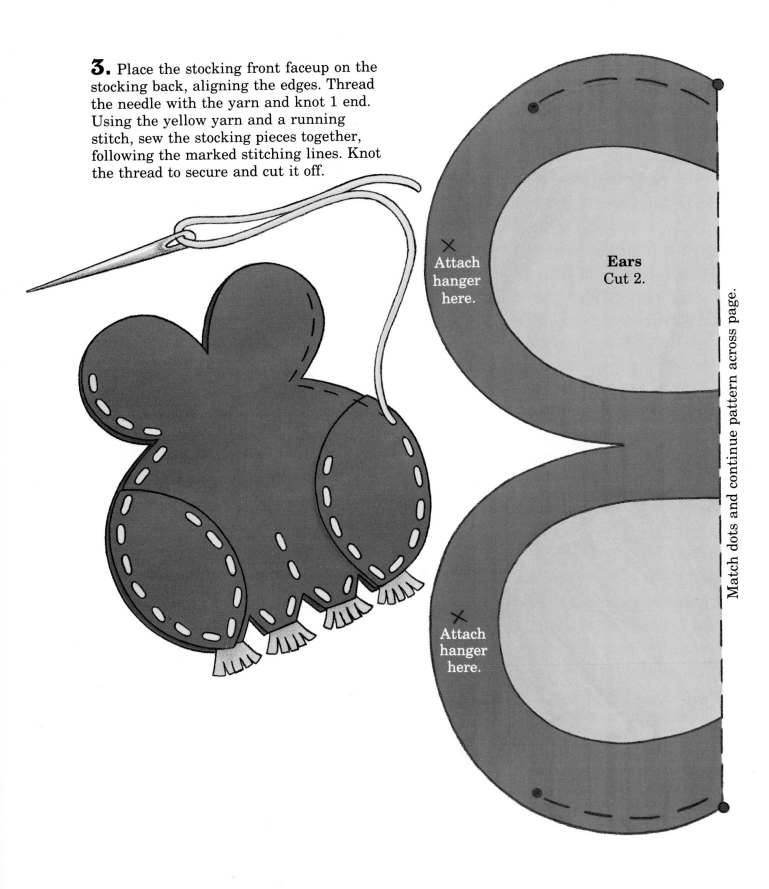

✕ Attach hanger here.

Ears
Cut 2.

✕ Attach hanger here.

Match dots and continue pattern across page.

112

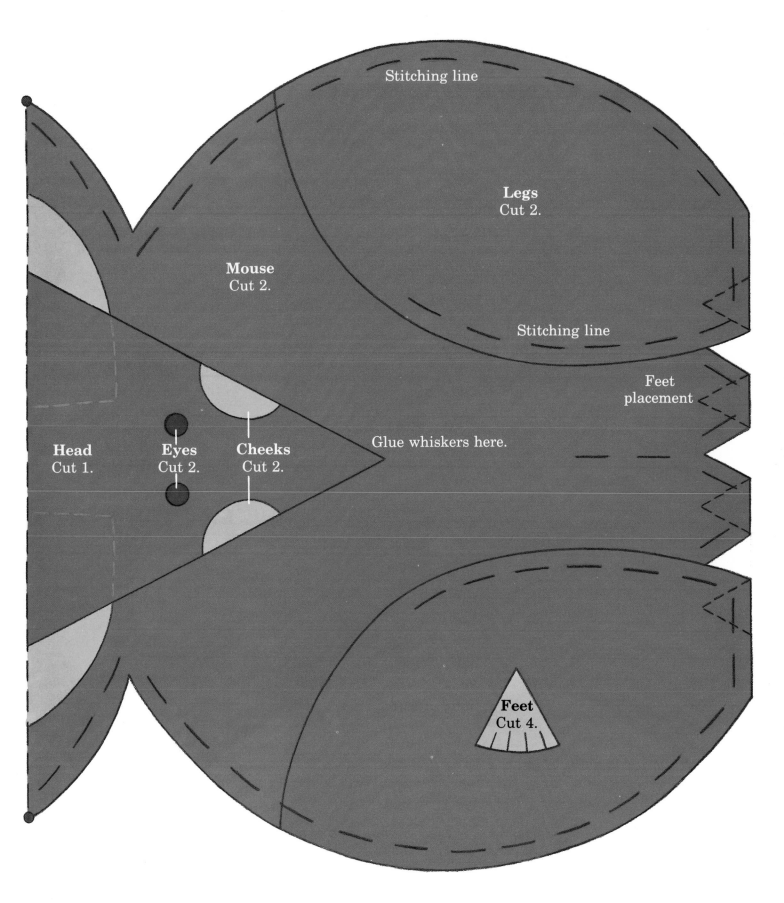

Stitching line

Legs
Cut 2.

Mouse
Cut 2.

Stitching line

Feet
placement

Glue whiskers here.

Head
Cut 1.

Eyes
Cut 2.

Cheeks
Cut 2.

Feet
Cut 4.

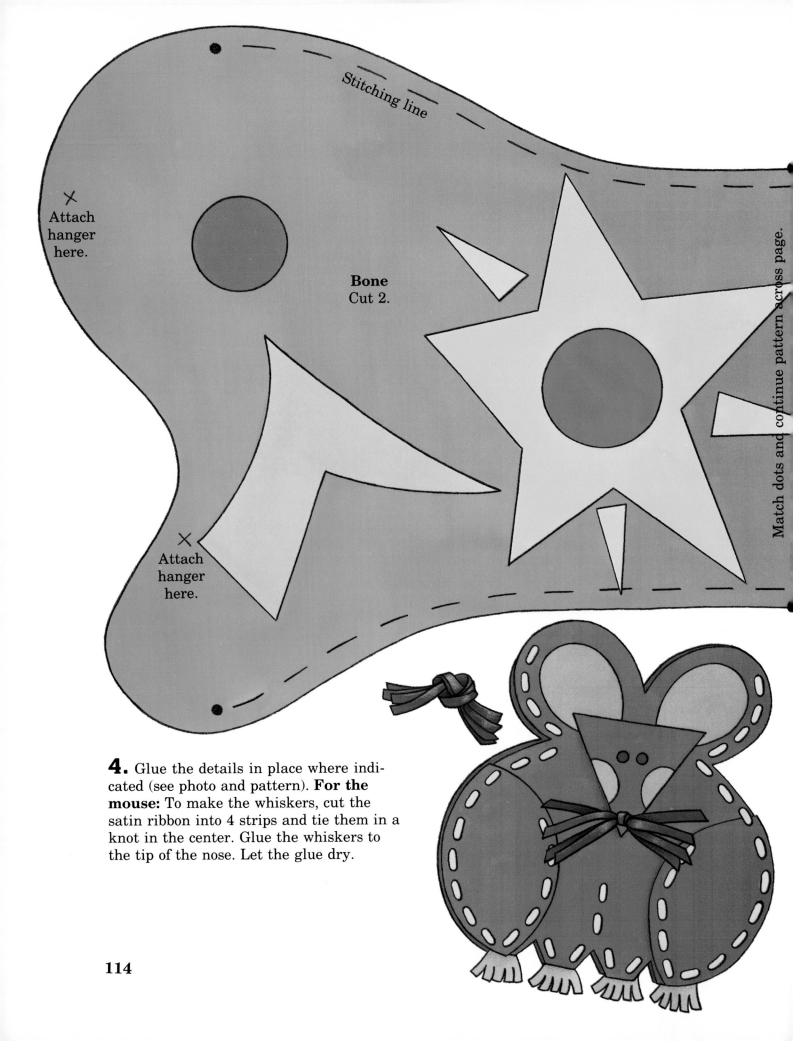

Stitching line

X
Attach
hanger
here.

Bone
Cut 2.

X
Attach
hanger
here.

Match dots and continue pattern across page.

4. Glue the details in place where indicated (see photo and pattern). **For the mouse:** To make the whiskers, cut the satin ribbon into 4 strips and tie them in a knot in the center. Glue the whiskers to the tip of the nose. Let the glue dry.

114

Stitching line

5. For the hanger, make 2 small holes in the back piece of felt where indicated on the pattern. Cut the cording into 3 (9″) strips and braid them together. Thread 1 end of the braided cording through each hole, forming a loop. Then tie a knot in each end to secure. Tie the ribbon into a bow around the hanger.

Lighten Up

Brighten any tree, mantel, staircase, or doorway with overgrown felt lights and rickrack cording. These bulbs are fun to make and to string along.

You will need:

Green jumbo rickrack (See Step 1 for length.)
Tracing paper
Pencil
Scissors
Felt: black, assorted colors
Fabric glue
Large safety pin

1. Before you begin, decide where you want to hang your garland. Cut a strip of rickrack to fit this space. Then determine how many lights you will need to hang on your garland.

2. Trace and cut out the patterns. Trace the patterns onto the felt to make as many lights as desired. Cut them out.

3. To make each light, stack 2 bulb pieces and glue them together around the edges. Let the glue dry. Center and glue the bulb to 1 long edge of the socket. Let the glue dry. Then fold the socket in half and glue the opposite edge to the other side of the bulb, leaving the sides unglued. Let the glue dry. Repeat to make remaining lights.

4. To string the lights, attach the safety pin to 1 end of the rickrack and guide it through the socket of each light.

Socket
Cut 1.

Bulb
Cut 2.

Here We Go Loop-De-Loop!

Making this merry-looking wreath is a cinch! Knot loops of gaily colored ribbon around a hoop. Then fasten jingle bells with satin bows to add a little shine.

You will need:
Ruler
9⅔ yards 1⅜"-wide cut-edge ribbon
Scissors
11"-diameter macramé hoop
3 yards satin ribbon
Jingle bells

1. Cut the cut-edge ribbon into pieces that are about 12" long.

2. Fold one ribbon in half to make a loop. Place the folded ribbon on top of the hoop, with the loop toward the inside (Drawing A). Place the cut ends of the ribbon together and bring them behind the hoop and through the loop in the ribbon (Drawing B). Place one ribbon end on top of the other and pull both ends to tighten the knot (Drawing C).

3. Loop and knot each ribbon in the same way, side by side, all the way around the hoop. When you have finished, pull apart the ends of the ribbons to make the wreath look fluffier.

4. Cut the satin ribbon into pieces that are about 18" long. String a jingle bell in the middle of each ribbon. Tie one ribbon to the hoop, between two knotted loops, and make a bow. Skip about five loops and tie another ribbon bow. Going around wreath, tie all satin ribbons into bows.

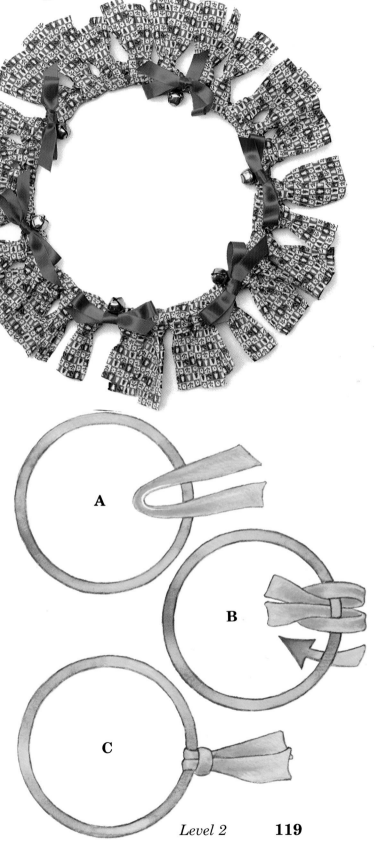

Sweet Street

Ask your mom if you can invite a friend over to make these houses with you. Building graham cracker houses is twice as easy—and twice the fun!— if you have four hands instead of two.

Before you start: Ask your mom to use the recipe on pages 31 and 32 to make the Royal Icing, but leave the icing white—do not add the food coloring.

You will need:
A grown-up
Graham cracker squares
Waxed paper
Bowl of Royal Icing (white)
Knife for spreading the icing
Index card
Scissors
Little candies
Miniature marshmallows
Tiny twigs
Black felt-tip marker
Green paste food coloring
Small bowl
Spoon
Sugar cones
Plastic snowflakes (the kind that you buy in a bag)

1. To make the walls of each house, lay one graham cracker on a sheet of waxed paper. Put icing around the edges of four other graham crackers. Stand them around the one that is on the waxed paper. Let the icing dry.

2. Use two graham crackers and icing to make a roof. Place it on top of the graham cracker walls.

3. From an index card, cut two triangles that are big enough to cover the holes at each end of the house. Spread icing on the triangles and then place them over the holes.

4. Cut windows and doors from graham crackers and "glue" them with icing onto the house. Decorate the house with more icing and a lot of little candies.

5. Make more houses. Set all of the houses aside to dry.

6. Put a bit of white icing between three miniature marshmallows to make the snowman. Use tiny round candies for earmuffs and tiny twigs for arms. Draw two dots for eyes with the black marker.

7. To make the sugar cone Christmas trees, place some of the white icing in a small bowl. Mix green paste food coloring with the icing. Spread the icing on the outside of the sugar cones. Shake candy sprinkles over the icing. Let the icing dry.

8. Set the houses, the snowman, and the trees on a table or a mantel. Make candy walkways. Then sprinkle the snowflakes.

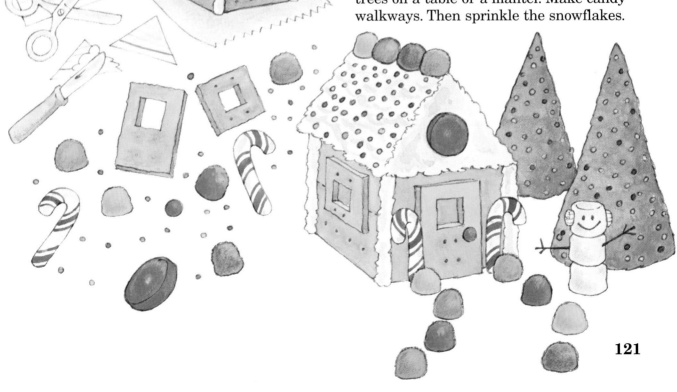

Santa Cones

All of these are the same except for one thing. Which beard do you think suits Santa best?

You will need:
Pencil
Tracing paper
Scissors
Pink, black, and yellow construction paper
Red party hat (or paper cone)
White glue
Hole punch
Tiny red heart sticker
Cotton
White construction paper (optional)
White reinforcement tabs (optional)
Ornament hanger

1. Trace and cut out the patterns for the face and boot. Cut out one pink face and two black boots. Glue the face to the hat. Glue the tops of the boots to the inside of the hat.

2. Punch two black circles for eyes and glue them to the face. Stick a heart sticker below the eyes. For the beard, glue on cotton, curled paper strips, or paper curly-cues, or stick on reinforcement tabs. Trim the hat with cotton.

3. Cut a black strip for Santa's belt and a yellow rectangle for the buckle. Glue the buckle to the belt. Glue the belt in place. Let the glue dry.

4. Hang Santa on the tree with the ornament hanger.

122   *Level 1*

Face

Boot

123

Stockings for Your Pet

Don't forget the family pets this Christmas. No bones about it—these stockings are purr-fect presents for them.

You will need (for each stocking):
Pencil
Tracing paper
Scissors
2 (8" x 10½") pieces of felt
Scraps of felt
Tacky craft glue
Small button for eye
Sewing needle and thread
Tape measure
Ribbon
Jingle bell
Paper for tag (optional)
Pom-pom
3 star sequins

1. Trace and cut out the patterns for the stocking.

2. Pin the body pattern to the 8" x 10½" pieces of felt. Cut out the pieces.

3. From felt, cut a nose, heart cheek, and mouth. Cut the pocket and the pocket trim. Cut a tail if you're making the cat.

4. Glue the nose, heart cheek, and mouth in place. Sew on the button eye.

5. Glue the pocket trim to the pocket. Put glue on the side and bottom edges of the pocket and position it on the stocking. Glue the cat's tail in place. Let the glue dry.

6. Thread the needle and tie the ends of the thread together. Using a running stitch, sew the body pieces together, following the broken lines on the pattern.

7. Cut a 28" piece of ribbon and thread the bell midway between the ends. Make a name tag if you like. Tie the ribbon around the pet stocking's neck.

8. Glue the pom-pom and the star sequins in place. Let the glue dry.

9. To make a loop for hanging, tie a piece of ribbon to the neck ribbon.

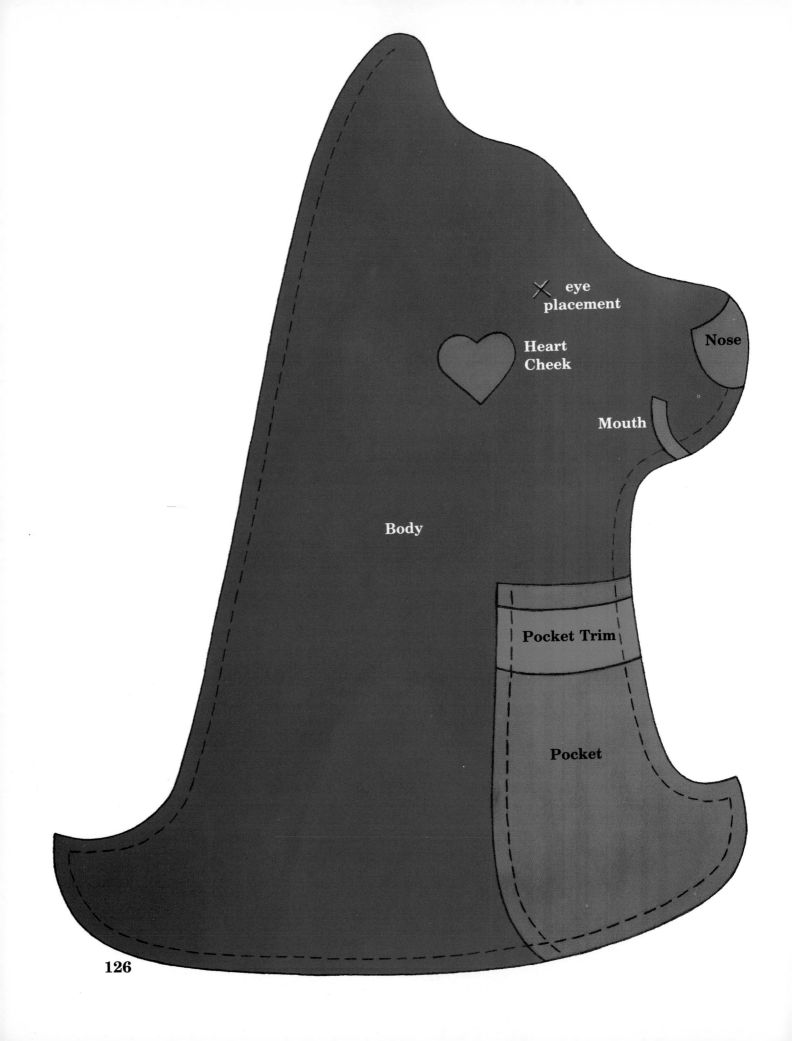

eye
placement

Nose

Heart
Cheek

Mouth

Body

Pocket Trim

Pocket

126

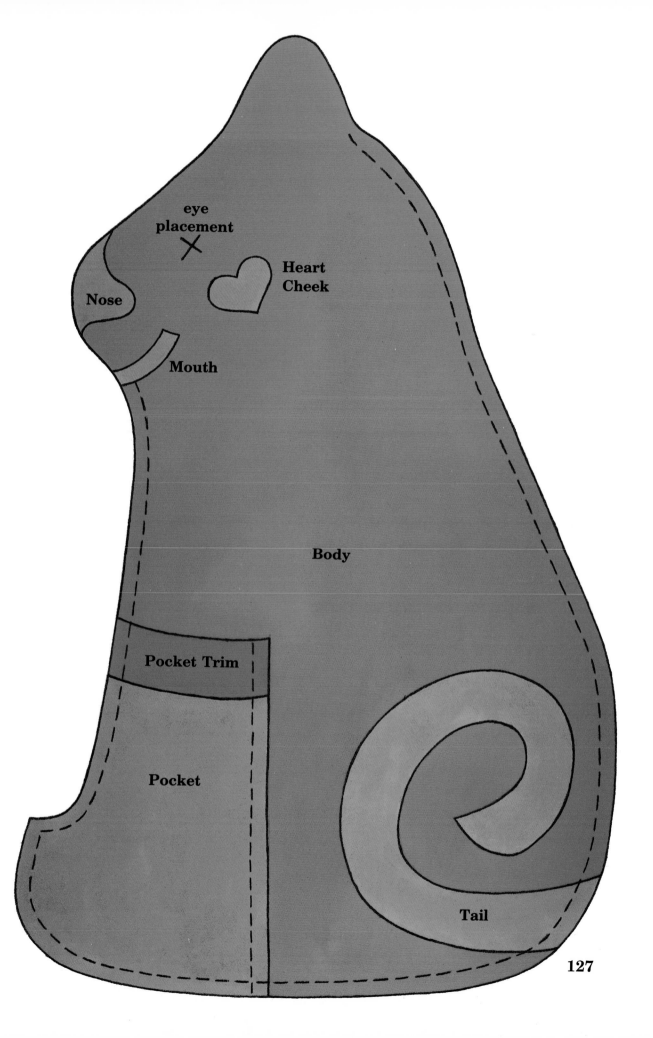

eye
placement

Heart
Cheek

Nose

Mouth

Body

Pocket Trim

Pocket

Tail

127

For the Door

Daffy Doormouse

Here's one mouse that Mom will welcome in the house! Tie him on a doorknob for a dandy decoration.

You will need:
Felt-tip marker
Small plate (about 7" in diameter)
Green felt
Scissors
Ruler
Hole punch
Top to mayonnaise jar
Tacky craft glue
Top to baby food jar
Red felt
2 plastic wiggly eyes
Narrow ribbon
Pom-pom

1. Draw around the plate on green felt. Cut out the felt circle. Using the hole punch, make holes that are 1″ apart around the circle, about 1″ from the edge.

2. Draw around the mayonnaise jar top four times on green felt. At the bottom of each felt circle, draw a tab that is 1″ long and 1½″ wide. Cut out the circles with the tabs attached.

3. Draw around the baby-food jar top two times on red felt. Cut out the felt circles.

4. For each ear, glue together two of the green felt circles with tabs. Glue a red felt circle on each ear.

5. Lay the ears in place on the felt circle with holes. Draw a line along the bottom of each ear tab. Cut along each line with your scissors.

6. Spread glue on the front of each ear tab. Put the tabs in the slits. Let the glue dry.

7. Glue on the wiggly-eyes. Cut six 2″ pieces of ribbon for whiskers. Put glue on one end of each ribbon. Glue the ribbon ends under the eyes. Glue a pom-pom nose on top of the ribbon ends. Let the glue dry.

8. Cut a piece of ribbon that is about 26″ long. Lace the ribbon through the holes.

9. Put the mouse on a doorknob. Pull the ends of the ribbon and tie a bow.

Candy Garland

Drape your doorway
with a gigantic "candy"
garland. Made from
Styrofoam bowls and
cellophane, this garland
should withstand even
a winter shower.

You will need:
16 (12-ounce) Styrofoam bowls
20″-wide colored cellophane: 5 feet each of
  blue, red, and green; 10 feet yellow
32 twist ties
8 feet of rope
16 gold pipe cleaners

1. Cut the blue, red, and green cellophane into 4 (20″ x 15″) pieces each. Cut the yellow cellophane into 8 (20″ x 15″) pieces. Cut the pipe cleaners in half.

2. Stack 2 pieces of yellow cellophane on a flat surface. Place the base of 1 bowl in the center and wrap both pieces of cellophane over the bowl. Twist each end of the cellophane tightly and secure with a twist tie. Repeat with the rest of the yellow cellophane and 3 more bowls.

3. Use just 1 piece of cellophane at a time to wrap each of the remaining bowls. Twist each end tightly and secure with a twist tie.

4. Lay the rope down on a flat surface. Beginning about 12″ from 1 end of the rope, start attaching the candy. Take 2 matching color bowls and place the flat rim sides together with the rope sandwiched in between them. To hold the bowls together and to attach them to the rope, wrap a pipe cleaner piece around the ends over the twist ties. Attach all the remaining bowls to the rope in the same way.

Deck the Doorknobs

All of the elves' doors have decorations much like these hanging from the knobs. They are quick, easy, and as much fun to make as toys!

You will need (for both hangers):
Tracing paper
Pencil
Scissors
Fun Foam: green, red, blue, yellow
¼"-diameter hole punch
Craft glue
For the bell hanger: ½ yard ½"-wide striped grosgrain ribbon

1. Trace the patterns onto the tracing paper. Cut them out.

2. Transfer the hanger base pattern once to the green foam and once to the red foam. Transfer the bell pattern onto the blue foam, the clapper and and star patterns onto the yellow foam, and the tree onto the green

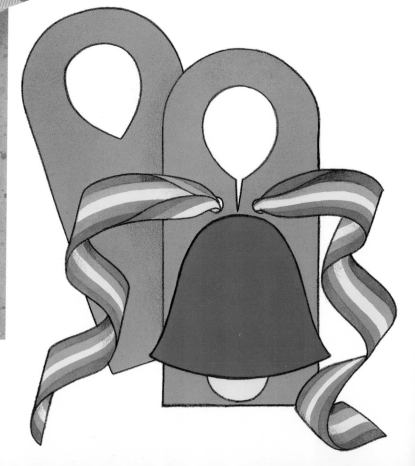

foam. Cut them out. Cut out the circle in the top of each hanger base, being careful not to cut from an outside edge. Using the hole punch, punch 10 dots from the blue foam and 8 dots from yellow foam scraps.

3. For the bell hanger: Referring to the photo, center and glue the clapper along the bottom of the green hanger base. Center and glue the bell above the clapper. Cut the slit on the hanger base where indicated on the pattern. Using the hole punch, punch holes in the hanger base where indicated on the pattern. Thread the ribbon through the holes and tie into a bow.

4. For the tree hanger: Referring to the photo, center and glue the tree to the red hanger base. Glue the star to the top of the tree. Glue the blue and yellow circles randomly on the tree and the hanger base. Cut the slit on the hanger base where indicated on the pattern.

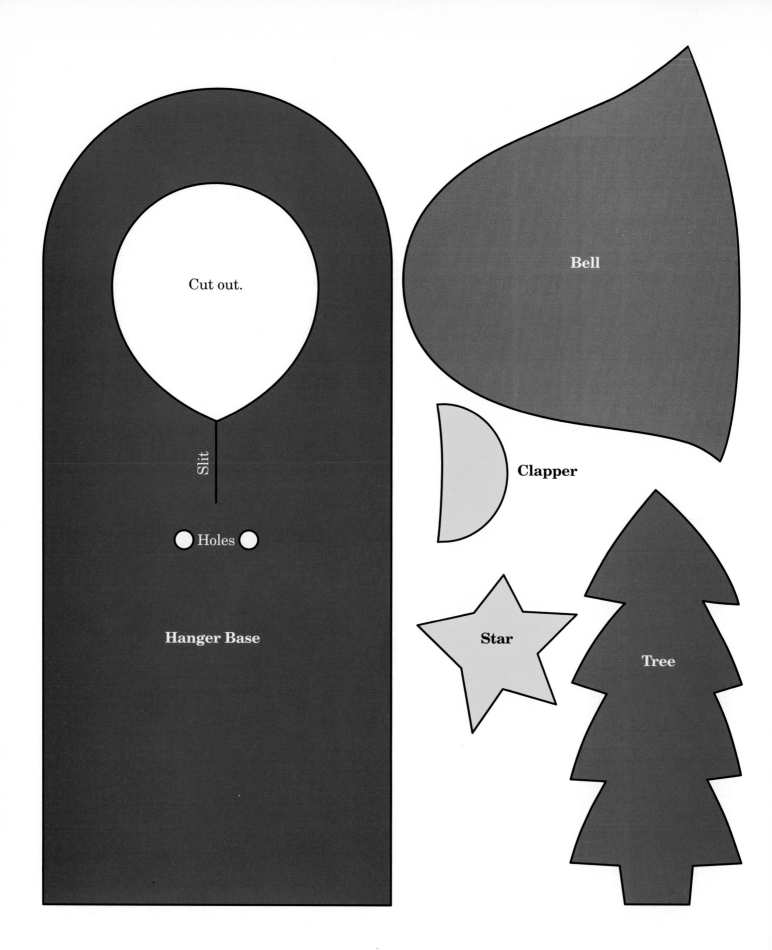

Cut out.

Slit

Holes

Hanger Base

Bell

Clapper

Star

Tree

Holiday Doorkeepers

Ready to welcome holidays and friends are a playful trio of Santa, an angel, and a snowman. Although they are made from extra-heavy paper plates, they still prefer to greet visitors indoors—winter winds are not their friends.

You will need (for each doorkeeper):

Waxed paper
2 (10½″) heavy-duty
    paper plates
Paintbrushes
White glue
Scissors
Stapler
Hole punch
20″ of thin cording
White glitter

For the angel:

Acrylic paints: yellow, pink
12″ piece of gold tinsel garland
18″ piece of ribbon
2 (⁷⁄₁₆″) blue buttons
1 (⅝″) pearl button
1 (½″) pink heart button
Gold glitter

For Santa:

Acrylic paints: red, pink, white
1 (2″) white pom-pom
2 (⅞″) black buttons
1 (1″) red glitter pom-pom
2 jingle bells

For the snowman:

Acrylic paints: turquoise, white, purple,
    green
1 (2″) white pom-pom
2 (1⅛″) black buttons
5 (½″) red buttons
3 (1″) orange pom-poms
2 jingle bells

Before you begin: Cover your work surface with waxed paper. When shaking off excess glitter, catch it on the waxed paper and put it back into the container.

Angel Doorkeeper

1. For the angel's neck, lightly mark off a 3″ section on the rim of 1 plate with a pencil. Cut away a 2″ piece on each side of the 3″ section.

2. Referring to the diagram, paint the angel's hair yellow and let it dry. Paint the face pink and let it dry.

3. Randomly spread a thin coat of glue on the angel's hair. Also spread glue on the cheeks. Sprinkle white glitter over these areas. Let the glue dry. Gently shake off the extra glitter.

4. For the halo, staple the ends of the garland to the rim of the plate. Staple the center of the ribbon to the collar and tie the ends to make a bow.

5. Glue on the button eyes, nose, and mouth. Let the glue dry.

6. From the other plate, cut 2 pie-shape sections for wings. Using a paintbrush, coat the wings with a thin layer of glue. Sprinkle them with gold glitter. Let the glue dry. Shake off the extra glitter. Staple the wings to the angel and cover the

staples with matching paint. Let them dry.

7. At the top of the plate, punch 2 holes about 6″ apart. For the hanger, tie several big knots at 1 end of the cording. From the back of the plate, thread the unknotted end of the cording through 1 of the holes. From the front of the plate, push the unknotted end of the cording through the other hole and knot the end.

Santa Doorkeeper

1. Paint the top third of 1 plate red for Santa's hat. Leave a 1¾″ strip unpainted for the hat trim. Paint the rest of the plate pink for the face. Let the paint dry.

2. Glue the white pom-pom on the hat trim and the button eyes on the face. Let the glue dry.

3. For Santa's beard, cut a 4½″-deep piece from the other plate. Staple it in place over the face. Paint the staples white. Glue on the red pom-pom nose and let it dry.

4. For the hanger, follow Step 7 in the directions for the angel but string the bells on the cording after the cording is thread through the first hole. Slide a bell down over each of the holes.

5. Using a paintbrush, spread a thin coat of glue on the cheeks and randomly on Santa's hat. Spread glue all over the hat trim and beard. Sprinkle glitter over these areas. Let the glue dry. Shake off the extra glitter.

140

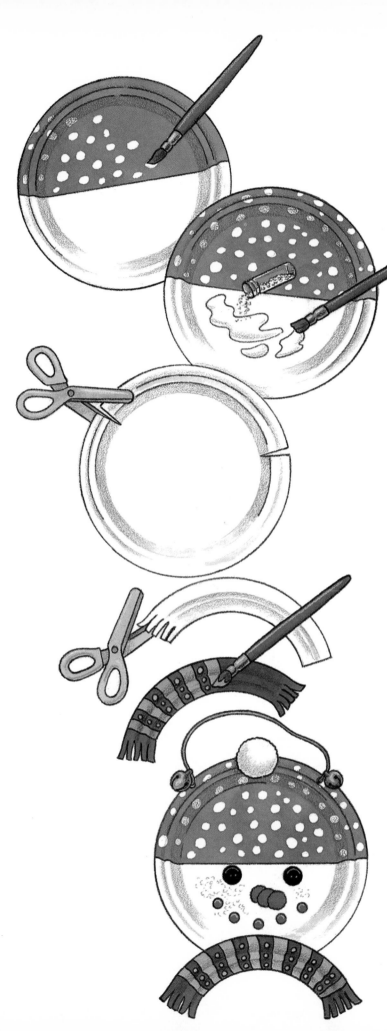

Snowman Doorkeeper

1. For the snowman's hat, paint the top half of 1 plate turquoise. Let it dry. Paint white polka dots on the hat and let them dry.

2. Using a paintbrush, spread a thin coat of glue on the polka dots and on the unpainted half of the plate (face). Sprinkle glitter over these areas and let it dry. Gently shake off the extra glitter.

3. Referring to the photo, glue on the white pom-pom, the button eyes, the button mouth, and 1 orange pom-pom nose. Let them dry. Glue another orange pom-pom on top of the first one. When it is dry, glue the third orange pom-pom to the second one and let it dry.

4. To make the scarf, cut a 10″ piece from the rim of the other plate. Cut the ends of the scarf with scissors to make fringe. Paint the scarf purple and let it dry. Then paint green stripes and polka dots. Let the paint dry. Staple the scarf to the snowman and paint over the staples with matching paint.

5. For the hanger, follow Step 7 in the directions for the angel but string the bells on the cording. Slide a bell down over each of the holes.

141

Handy-Dandy Door Decoration

Here's a super idea for sprucing up your classroom door.

Level 1

You will need:
8½" x 11" sheets of green paper
Pencils
Scissors
Paper and tape for covering door
Glue stick
Paper for cutouts

1. Give a sheet of green paper to each of your classmates.

2. Ask everyone to draw around his or her hand on the paper, as shown, and cut them out.

3. Cover your classroom door with paper.

4. Fold the paper hands about 2" from the straight edges. Glue the folded edge of each hand to the door so that the hands make a tree.

5. Decorate the tree and the door with paper cutouts.

Designers & Contributors

Chere Brodsky, Cookie-Cutter Kids, 88

Marilyn M. Carlton, Paint Stick Ornaments, 52

Peyton Carmichael, Dip-and-Drape Angel, 14

Sharon Christman, Color Melts, 34

Kim Eidson Crane, Picture-Perfect Wreaths, 26; Surprise Balls, 59; Nutty Reindeer Ornaments (concept by **Rina Albala**), 72; Daffy Doormouse, 130; Candy Garland, 132

Phyllis Dunstan, Wire Stars, 38

Connie Formby, Window Wonderland, 84

Janelle Hayes, Everything That Glitters, 45

Linda Hendrickson, Merry Mice, 8; Glitter Birds, 22; Nursery Rhyme Ornaments, 48; Peppermint Ponies, 86; Jumping Jack, 90; Stockings for Your Pet, 110; Pet Stockings, 124

Heidi Tyline King, Lighten Up, 116; Deck the Doorknobs, 134

Eve London, Glitter Ornaments, 78

Dot Renneker, Sweet Street, 120

Janet A. Rubino, Oodles of Noodles, 66

Trés Rush, Wee Weavings, 11

Betsy Cooper Scott, Christmas Tree Skirt, 62; Sugarplum Trees, 106

Joan M. Sleeth, Glittery Snowflakes, 65

Linda Martin Stewart, Powder-Puff Snowmen, 18; Just Ducky!, 60; Spoon Angel, 69; Holiday Doorkeepers, 137

Robin D. Snyder, Dream Cones, 24

Kathleen A. Taylor, Here We Go Loop-De-Loop!, 119

Karen T. Tillery, Seeing Stars, 56

Carol M. Tipton, Animal Zoobilee, 74; Paper Plate Angel, 81; Away in a Manger, 94

DeeDee Triplett, Ribbon Candy, 70

Cynthia Moody Wheeler, Fun Foam Forest, 102

Madeline O'Brien White, Shiny Shapes, 20; Take-the-Cake Cupcakes, 31; Pop-Silly-Sicles, 42; Treasures from Trash, 46; Sweet Street, 120; Santa Cones, 122

Special thanks to the following shops in Birmingham, Alabama, for sharing their resources with *Christmas is Coming!*: **Chocolate Soup, Inc.; Jack N' Jill Shop; Sikes Children's Shoes.**